Everyone Dies!

Secrets That Can
Save You Thousands in
Unnecessary Funeral Costs.

Handbook
For
The Informed Family

An in-depth resource guide that provides valuable information about
funeral services and the many options available.

By Ralph Hicks

Former funeral director and owner/manager of multiple
funeral homes and a cemetery operation.

Disclaimer

Equitable Associates is not a funeral director or in any way associated with the funeral industry. **Equitable Associates** is a funeral resource consultant and a shopping service. **Equitable Associates** receives no commission or percentage for any service or merchandise that it might recommend. All financial arrangements or contracts with recommended companies are between the client and the recommended company the client chooses.

The Publisher
R & B Enterprises
P.O. Box 1741
Ruidoso, NM 88355-1741

First Edition ☐ January 1999

ISBN   0-9669695-0-2

Library of Congress Catalog Card Number: 99-93016

For :

My beloved mother, Ina M. Hicks, who taught me
about living and through her death about dying.

I dedicate this book to her memory —
she would have been proud!

Ralph

Understanding Funeral
Terms & Language

What They Called It Then	What They Call It Now
Ashes	Cremains
Body	Deceased or decedent. Also referred to by Mr., Mrs., Miss, or Ms. _____
Burial of ashes	Inurnment
Burial plot salesperson	Family Service Counselor
Bury	Inter
Casket showroom	Display room
Cemetery operator	Cremeterian
Coffin	Casket
Cost of casket and burial	Investment in the service
Dead	Expired
Embalming	Creating a memory picture
Embalming Room	Preparation room
Embalming School	Colleges of mortuary science
Funeral	Service
Funeral Job	Call
Graveyard	Cemetery or memorial gardens
Putting the body in the casket	Casketing
Putting the casket in a mausoleum	Immuring
Removing the body	Transfering
Retort	Cremation chamber
Undertaker or mortician	Funeral Director

Table of Contents

Please send me _____ copies of the book:

Everyone Dies!

**Secrets That Can
Save You Thousands in
Unnecessary Funeral Costs.**

Name: _____

Company Name: _____

Address: _____

City: _____ State: _____ Zip: _____

Telephone: (   ) _____

Enclosed is a check or money order for $19.95 plus $3.75 shipping & handling for first book and $2.00 for each additional book.

New Mexico residents, please add 6.9375% sales tax ($1.25) per book.

Send to:

Equitable Associates
P.O. Box 1741
Ruidoso, NM 88355-1741

OR

Call toll free 1-888-556-1350 to place your order.

Credit Card Orders: Web Site
http://www.adelegate.com

1

Who We Are

About the Company

Equitable Associates, LLC, was formed to provide people with information and research materials that will help them avoid overly inflated funeral goods and services. We provide shopping services through a network of businesses that provide quality goods and services at equitable prices.

Equitable Associates is a consulting company created to give you money-saving secrets and alternatives for doing what you desire to honor and respect your loved one. You may not always receive these alternatives from your local funeral director, mortuary or cemetery.

We are all very different in life, and we are all different in what we want at the time of our death. Some are religious; some are not. Some want earth burial, and some want cremation. Some might want to be buried in a suit, because that's what most people remember them wearing during life. Perhaps others would look more natural in overalls, or golf and tennis attire or whatever.

If your loved one attended a church, perhaps a Memorial Service would be more appropriate in the church or mortuary chapel. But what if your loved one was not religious? Perhaps the local golf club would be more appropriate for the Memorial Service or where the service club meets. What about a park or in your back yard, for the Memorial Service, with friends being able to talk about the good times, or a funny story, or how your loved one helped them fix their car, etc.

Death is the conclusion of this life. And if the intent of a Memorial Service, is to honor your loved one, it may be held in surroundings that had been comfortable to the deceased or loved one, as well as provide some healing for friends and relatives that are left behind.

Equitable Associates help you to understand your rights as a consumer of funeral goods and services based on the ruling by the Federal Trade Commission (FTC) called the Funeral Rule; that went into effect April 30, 1984, a copy of which will be sent to you upon request.

OUR GOALS:

➤ To provide current and factual information in verbal and written form. We provide you with the questions to ask the funeral director, mortuary or cemetery, *before or immediately after* the death of your loved one.

➤ To explain the traditional funeral process from the time death occurs until burial or cremation. We will then show you the step-by-step process that funeral directors goes through on your behalf and how they charge for each step in the process. We will show you the steps you can do yourself, or with the help of friends to save some of these expenses.

➤ To suggest things that you can do as a family that could save you money.

➤ To shop on your behalf at the funeral homes in your area for competitive prices.

➢ We will provide you with names of companies that sell caskets, and other burial-related merchandise, so that you can buy direct and save several hundreds of dollars.

➢ Our shopping service will put you in contact with businesses in your area that can save you up to 50% on cemetery lots versus buying lots at the cemetery.

➢ To help you save hundreds of dollars in unwanted services. We can help ease the pressures at this very difficult time because we will provide you with reliable information that, heretofore, were secrets of the funeral industry.

➢ Help you to implement *your* ideas to honor your loved one, and to keep the ceremony as inexpensive and simple as desired, while maintaining dignity and respect.

➢ Help you with pre-arranged funeral planning, where *you* keep control of your money, by using *your own bank!*

Funeral service has always been a *"for-profit"* business, and in most cases the local funeral home endeavored to provide excellent service at a fair price. However, over the last few years I have seen a drastic change in funeral service.

Large funeral and cemetery conglomerates have purchased family funeral homes. After the purchase, the conglomerate keeps the family name on the outside of the building, but management and the prices are set from corporate headquarters, not in your home town.

My research has shown that you can receive equitable prices in today's high priced funeral market.

TODAY'S COSTS for a	VS.	EQUITABLE PRICE for a

Traditional Funeral with a
Metal Casket *(Non-Sealing)*

$3,000 to $10,000

Direct Cremation

$750 to $4,000

Metal Casket only, *(Non-Sealing)*

$1,000 to $6,000

Traditional Funeral with a
Metal Casket *(Non-Sealing)*

$1,500 to $2,500

Direct Cremation

$360 to $600

Metal Casket only, *(Non Sealing)*

$500 to $900

Individual consulting, as well as our shopping service is available by calling **Equitable Associates**. We know all the ins and outs of funeral arrangements, and can "walk" you through each step with an eye toward getting your money's worth and an equitable price.

<u>**All of our recommendations are without commission.**</u>
<u>**We put you in contact with each vendor or funeral home to make**</u>
<u>**your own financial arrangements**</u>.

Available 24 hours a day.

Call our toll free pager 1-888-556-1350

Our Guarantee

If you are not completely satisfied with our services, we will gladly refund our fees.

2

Protect Your Emotions
&
Your Pocketbook

Since death comes at all hours, and often suddenly, we will address arranging a funeral from several angles. First, we'll take the worst-case scenario wherein death has come unexpectedly. You must act quickly and make decisions that will determine not only the quality and the cost of the funeral, but how you and the family will be regarded later by others and yourselves.

This starts with the notification of death and covers all the basics. Next, we will look into the funeral industry at a more leisurely pace to examine all the options available and how to hold costs to a reasonable level, while still providing the dignity and respect we expect. This applies principally to situations in which you have advance warning of impending death and have time to plan.

Finally, we'll examine how one goes about pre-planning his or her own or loved one's funeral, and the options available. We will provide you with work sheets for you to fill out to let your survivors know what you expect and desire.

At each step we'll look at ways you can save on costs or get more for your money. We'll also examine **common ploys** used to entice you to spend more than you really should, and often perpetuated against families who are vulnerable and emotional following the loss of a loved one.

No one wants to dwell upon the unpleasant, but by the same token no one wants to be put in the position of having to make highly personal financial decisions in the blind either. The more you know, and the more you know what to ask for, the less additional stress you'll have to contend with when the time comes, and, it will come for us all.

This information is not intended to impugn the reputation of those in the industry, but rather help to educate the consumer at a very difficult time in their life. The funeral industry does have its share of outright scoundrels, and more than a few (perhaps the majority) will charge, **whatever the market will bear**, for their goods and services. This is expected when dealing with a population that, for the most part, does not want to talk about death, who do not know the questions to ask at the time of death, and have thought of the funeral industry as being secretive and mysterious. Our intent and desire is to provide you with **KNOWLEDGE**, which is power that can help you during this difficult situation.

Don't Make Arrangements Alone

Heart attacks, strokes, auto accidents, violence, suicide, drowning; a host of forms of sudden death assails us and leaves those who cared for him or her stunned. It is during this period of shock that many of the most important decisions relating to the funeral arrangements must be made by the deceased's family. The funeral director, on the other hand, deals with this sort of thing every day and has the immense psychological advantage of viewing the deceased as **business**. For this reason, the very first principle in arranging any funeral is:

> **PRINCIPLE # 1   Don't go alone!**

Before you approve the first step such as releasing the body to a funeral home or identifying the remains, get someone you know and can trust, and preferably someone not related to or emotionally involved with the deceased, and talk. It would help if this person has been through the process of arranging a funeral, and would help even more if they had been through it recently themselves.

Things will happen quickly over the first few hours, only if you allow them. While you're waiting for your friend to join you, consider this: The deceased will be no worse off if you take a few minutes to make some phone calls or to confer with your friend. You could make costly snap decisions at the funeral directors guided questions such as, *"Will it be burial or cremation?"* Or, *"May we suggest the **Standard Package?"*** Or, *"I know you'd want only the **VERY BEST** for your loved one"*. You could relinquish your decision-making power to the funeral director *"Just leave **everything** to us"* and **YOU** could live to regret it for years. You can **BUY TIME** in most cases, and you should do just that!

Your Need for a Trusted Friend or Consultant

The sudden death/short notice funeral is the most challenging to arrange due to time constraints and the decisions that must be made while still in something of an emotional state of shock. You are extremely vulnerable at this time and it is far too easy for a soft-spoken salesperson to lead you down an expensive path at this time.

Hence, the need for a friend or consultant with a level head to accompany you every step of the way. One sales training tactic recommended to trainees is, "If you can get them crying, you can get them to buy". And, some are not beyond using words and phrases to elicit emotion. Reality must remain in the forefront during negotiations on the arrangements. The funeral is a method of saying goodbye and disposing of the remains.

The difference between crepe and a velvet lining in a casket won't matter to the departed, nor will the bronze, copper, steel or wood exterior of the casket, nor the plastic handles on the vault, or the view from the gravesite. What will matter, and what will be remembered by all, will be the caring and the support received by family and friends and the lasting memory of your loved one.

Set a reasonable budget and insist the funeral director stay within it. Spend your time with loved ones and friends, not worrying about paying the bills.

Remember that time can be your enemy in the sudden death scenario. There will be a temptation to just throw up your hands and let the funeral director make all the decisions because of time pressures, uncomfortable questions, uncomfortable decisions, uncomfortable surroundings and the added emotional stress of the overwhelming amount of details that need to be attended to at this time. But, letting the funeral director make all the arrangements could be very expensive on many levels and for years to come. At this time you are in a very vulnerable state and could be easily led due to your emotional state and lack of knowledge about the funeral business.

Take the time to get yourself equitable prices on funeral goods and services. Should you encounter anything that you need help with, don't hesitate to call **Equitable Associates**. We can be the friend that you can lean on at such a desperate time. We know the industry and can help you by getting the information you need to save money and guide you through the process.

Your Friend, and Ally

<u>Remember the 1st Principle? Never go alone!</u>

Okay, so who will it be? It must be someone whose judgement you trust, someone with enough spirit to say "No" or at least "Not yet", and someone you can reach in an instant and remain close to you for several days. That may narrow your choice down considerably. Also, you may want to keep in mind that too many people helping could cause more confusion.

Select a couple of possibilities and prioritize them. Ideally you'll want someone a bit removed from the deceased, for objectivity, and someone who has been through the funeral arrangement process within the past few years, for experience. Beyond this you'll want a friend.

Make your best picks and let them help when the time comes. As you now realize, there's lots of decisions to make and lots of things to remember. For that reason, two minds are better on the job than one.

U. S Death Statistics: 1960 – 2080

Year	U.S. Population	Number of U.S. Deaths	Death Rate Per 1000 Population
1960	179,323,000	1,711,982	9.55
1970	203,302,000	1,921,031	8.45
1980	229,302,000	1,989,841	8.78
1985	238,736,000	2,086,440	8.74
1990	248,709,873	2,162,000	8.6
1991	252,160,000	2,165,000	8.5
1992	255,082,000	2,177,000	8.5
1993	261,000,000	2,268,000	8.8
1994	261,500,000	2,286,000	8.8
1995	264,396,000	2,309,000	8.8
1996	265,200,000	2,311,000	8.7
1997	266,788,000	2,294,000	8.6
2000 P	268,266,000	2,367,000	8.82
2010 P	282,575,000	2,634,000	9.32
2020 P	294,364,000	3,015,000	10.24
2030 P	300,629,000	3,472,000	11.55
2040 P	310,807,000	4,100,000	12.85
2050 P	299,849,000	4,100,000	13.67
2060 P	296,963,000	3,912,000	13.17
2070 P	294,642,000	3,832,000	13.01
2080 P	292,235,000	3,814,000	13.05

Source: National Funeral Directors Association

3

What To Do
With The Body

The first question asked after learning of the of death of a loved one will likely be, *"What shall we do with the body?"* **Do not be in a hurry to move the body!**

Depending on the time of day and other factors, your best answer to authorities (such as hospitals, nursing homes, and perhaps police officers, etc.) will most likely be *"Please keep (him, her) until I can firm-up arrangements."* This response is expected and rarely causes conflicts. Remember that **death may come suddenly, but the arrangements should follow in an orderly progression.** Haste definitely means waste, in financial terms, and allowing authorities to rush you will add even more stress to an already stressful situation.

If Death Occurred In A Nursing Home:

If the death occurred in a nursing home, retaining the body may not be an option since some, perhaps most, nursing homes do not have the facilities for storing bodies indefinitely, and they likely have someone waiting for the bed. This is not to say they can't hold the body for a few hours while you make arrangements. **Do not be pressured into an immediate decision**. If pressed, you can simply say that you think the deceased may have a burial plan with one of the funeral homes, but you aren't certain which one and will need to check before authorizing the transfer of the body.

Most likely the deceased bed is paid for through the end of the month, so don't feel bad about making them wait a few hours to fill it. *You may also ask for a refund for the unused time.*

If Death Occurred In A Hospital:

Most hospitals have morgues in their pathology unit and can retain the deceased for several days, if need be. Their rates should be reasonable if not *free of charge*. This is not required but contrasted with the inflated storage charges at many funeral homes who charge several hundreds of dollars, it can be a viable option. **Ask!**

If Death Occurred At Home:

Even if the death occurred at home, there is a strong likelihood the body will be transported to the local hospital or city morgue/medical examiner's office as a matter of custom or law. Unless the death was accidental, homicide, or suicide, an autopsy **will not** generally be performed.

If Death Occurred In Another City:

Deal with only ONE funeral home **(usually the one in the city where the deceased will be buried).** It is not uncommon to die in a different city. Given the medical community's desire to transfer to the most advanced facility in the region, the hospital, coroner's office, police department or even a minister or priest may recommend or suggest a funeral home in the city where the death occurred. In this case you could be paying for duplicate services.

In any event, unless you have detailed prior plans for the funeral, **do not be in a hurry to move the body**. You'll learn why shortly.

The time that you take to assess your situation can be valuable since it delays pressing the decision on which funeral home, if any, will receive the deceased. This can mean a difference of $1,000.00 or more in funeral expenses due to the ability to **Shop** the various funeral homes and avoid unnecessary or duplicate fees. Which brings us now to Principle #2.

PRINCIPLE #2   Deal with ONLY ONE funeral home.

This principle is paramount because whoever informs you of the death may recommend or suggest a funeral home that charges exorbitant fees and services that you may not want.

In each funeral arrangement there are such things as Receiving Charges, Preparation Charges, Transportation Charges, and the **NON-DECLINABLE FEES.**

Non-declinable charges are also known as "Fees for Professional Services". These are fixed rates you must pay that usually cover the overhead of the funeral home and are usually listed "Basic Services", "Professional Services", "Services of Funeral Director & Staff", etc., on the funeral home's General Price List. All other genuine services are extra, such as transporting the body to the funeral home, embalming, body preparations, encasing the body in either a shipping tray or a combination tray, and delivery to the airport for shipment.

If Death Occurred Out-of-State

Fares for transportation are extra, and the law requires the body to be embalmed if traveling by a **common carrier** such as an airline or any vehicle where the body would come in close proximity to other humans. Bear in mind that hearses and the funeral home utility vehicles are **NOT** considered common carriers. When bodies are transported in a hearse or utility vehicle, **embalming is always optional even *when they cross state lines.*** There are only a few exceptions.

It is not uncommon for non-declinable fees to run $1,000 or more. Here's the catch. Say you live in Los Angeles and your loved one died in New York. The authorities might recommend a funeral director in New York to help you with the transportation of the body to the funeral home in Los Angeles where the actual burial will take place. The funeral director in New York will likely charge you the "Forwarding of Remains Fee (which is a non-declinable fee). You will, in all probability, have to **pay this same charge again** when the body is received at the funeral home in Los Angeles under "Receiving Remains from Another Funeral Home. And it's all proper and legal.

Avoid duplication of Non-Declinable Fees. Many of the packages offered by funeral homes may include things that you have already paid for from the forwarding funeral home or for things that you may not need for your particular situation. Incidentally, the

---

PRINCIPLE #3   DO NOT agree to have the deceased transported to a funeral home, *unless* that is where the funeral and burial services will take place.

---

forwarding funeral home is required to send it's General Price List with the Invoice to the receiving funeral home in order for you to know what you have paid for and to allow you to scrutinize the charges. This can be very overwhelming and confusing if you are not familiar with the workings of this industry. **Equitable Associates** can help you by finding an equitable price in most situations.

The savings can easily amount to $1,000 or more by your not paying duplicate fees for services already rendered at each end particularly when your loved one dies in another state.

IT IS ESSENTIAL THAT YOU READ THE FINE PRINT TO SEE WHAT YOU ARE PAYING FOR UNDER EACH CATEGORY ON THE GENERAL PRICE LIST.

When death occurs out of state the situation lends itself to added expense because of the usage of two funeral homes and transportation charges. Some people might explore the possibility of burial in another state or cremation in the state where the death occurred as an alternative.

Food For Thought

If we were to die Monday through Friday, with one funeral a day, and two weeks off for the funeral directors vacation, the following chart shows the number of funeral homes that would be needed in each state, compared to the actual number. There are undoubtedly some funeral homes that can handle more than one funeral a day, which reduces the "needed" number accordingly and probably explains the figures for California, Hawaii, and Nevada.

Certainly in rural areas with sparse population, a funeral home does not expect the dying business to be a full-time one, and more establishments will be needed to cover the geographic area than the number generated by a single death-rate formula. In most other states, however, the number of funeral homes far exceeds that which can be reasonably supported by the death rate. (In Kansas, Pennsylvania, and Vermont, there are almost four times the needed funeral homes; in Iowa and Nebraska, there are five times too many!)

Why are so many funeral homes still in business? Because of high mark-ups that consumers pay either willingly or **because they just don't know what their options are.** It's a situation that invites pricing abuse.

State	Needed	Existing	State	Needed	Existing
AL	173	363	MO	221	707
AK	11	19	MT	31	87
AZ	146	134	NE	62	290
AR	108	286	NV	52	31
CA	904	757	NH	37	103
CO	101	167	NJ	291	790
CT	117	325	NM	52	66
DE	25	77	NY	661	1981
DC	27	40	NC	266	686
FL	621	794	ND	24	110
GA	237	660	OH	427	1271
HI	31	21	OK	133	355
ID	34	77	OR	115	161
IL	430	1388	PA	571	1881
IN	206	700	RI	38	127
IA	116	582	SC	135	392
KS	96	332	SD	27	135
KY	149	495	TN	207	475
LA	162	333	TX	563	1201
ME	47	158	UT	44	97
MD	166	263	VT	20	70
MA	220	724	VA	211	474
MI	334	805	WA	165	195
MN	150	498	WV	82	289
MS	109	315	WI	180	590
			WY	15	35

Source: Mortality rates for 1995-6. Center for Disease Control and a report of established funeral homes taken from 1993 and 1996 figures in the National Directory of Morticians (corrected in some states). It is likely that the figures for the numbers of existing funeral homes are approximate only and may be higher. Information supplied by Funerals and Memorial Societies of America.

4

Overview of
Choices for Funerals

Okay, the hospital called (you have your friend at your side) and you've told them to hold the body until arrangements are made. Now, how do you go about making these arrangements?

First, you decide what services you will need. To determine this, you must think past the funeral to the **"final disposition of remains"**, that is, where the body will come to rest. Will your choice be *Cremation with a Service? Immediate Cremation? Immediate Burial? Burial with a Service? Mausoleum? or Donation?*

Let's consider each since the end result will dictate much in the way of what you will need a funeral home to do, if indeed you need a funeral home at all. Did you know that in most states funeral directors are not required. You could have the option of transporting the body yourself...See March 23, 1998 U.S. News & World Report, page 55, "A home funeral for her husband."

Cremation with a Service:

This is where you have a traditional funeral service with the body present. It is required that the body is embalmed before viewing takes place at the funeral chapel or church of your choice. After the services, the body is then transported to the crematory for cremation.

Immediate Cremation:

This is also known as **Direct Cremation**. A direct cremation is usually when the body is not embalmed and as soon as the burial permit is secured, the body is transported to the crematory for cremation. <u>No viewing of the body is involved.</u> It is conceivable that in one trip a body could be picked up from the place of death, secure the death certificate, get the permit, transport to the crematory and the body NEVER gets to the funeral home. I, personally, have done this BUT the timing has to be just right. Under normal circumstances, the body is at the funeral home just long enough for the family to sign the cremation authorization and the burial permit secured before the body is taken to the crematory.

If you decide on direct cremation call the nearest crematory or several if possible. Inquire about prices and services. It is not uncommon for costs to vary widely within a given area. One city where I recently checked prices had several funeral homes. One funeral home's price sheet listed direct cremation with alternative container for **$1,085,** but did not include the cremation fee. In the same area a crematory priced a direct cremation for **$495** which included the cremation fee; a **savings of $590.** Keep your eyes open. Paying just *once* for services can save you money.

Burial with a Service:

This is a traditional funeral service. At the funeral home the body is embalmed and prepared for viewing and visitation and a funeral service. The funeral service can take place at the funeral home chapel or a church or synagogue, followed by a procession to the cemetery for burial or to a mausoleum for immurement or any combination of this process.

Immediate Burial:

This is also known as direct burial. In most cases the burial takes place within 48 hours after death. Usually, the funeral home puts the body in a casket and transports it to a cemetery of choice. There is no embalming and, in most cases, no viewing takes place because the body is not embalmed.

If you decide on a direct burial, the remains are taken directly from the place of death or morgue to the cemetery with, perhaps, a short stop at the funeral home until the burial permit is secured and the cemetery lot is purchased.

Embalming is optional providing no common carrier is involved. There are only a handful of states, which actually **require embalming** (and some only in cases of death from a communicable disease), so don't be bullied into this. It's the law!

In fact, part of the recent legislation plainly states that funeral homes are not to misrepresent state laws on embalming, but it may be up to you to stress this when the funeral home representative gets to his calculator and charge sheets. Enforcement of these laws is slack at best and when I have called to price shop a funeral home, I have been told repeatedly that "The State requires embalming" when it is not true. So be careful and protect your rights.

You can check with the Funeral Directors and Embalmers License Board of your state, but know that the majority of the board members are funeral directors. Or, you can call us at **Equitable Associates** and we can obtain that information for you.

Mausoleum:

These are buildings for above-ground burials. The buildings house concrete structures with marble facings, called crypts. Some mausoleums are very large buildings completely enclosed with many corridors containing hundreds of crypts. Others are outside structures that have no overhead coverings, just walls of crypts within the mausoleum. Some larger indoor mausoleums are even decorated with furniture, paintings for the comfort of the visitors. They also provide places for mementos of the deceased to be placed in front of the crypt.

The price of the crypts depends upon the location. The locations usually have names such as Kneeling Level, Eye Level, Highest Level, Heart Level etc., with Eye Level being the most expensive.

You have choices of single crypts, some are placed end to end for two people. Some are placed side by side for two people. They also have what is called a "couch", in which the casket is placed in the crypt sideways. Some mausoleum crypts can sell for as high as $15,000, with the average being somewhere between $1,000 to $2,500 per crypt. Usually buying the companion crypts, (end to end or side by side) are less expensive per crypt than buying two single crypts.

The cemetery will charge an opening/closing of the crypt, as well as a charge for the bronze nameplate. You may also be charged for a flower vase.

Most of the mausoleums offer flower preparation areas nearby with water to accommodate the families. Incidentally, the pungent scent in the building comes from the wide variety of fresh flowers present at any given time.

Donation of Body to Medical Science:

Another option is donate the body to science. Many funeral directors try to avoid this option, and will not always tell you the truth about donation due to their own greed. Several funeral directors have told families of prospective donors that medical schools are refusing bodies. Or they'll say that, *" Since your loved one was advanced in age, a victim of cancer, or heart failure, male or female, overweight,* (pick an excuse) the medical schools and teaching hospitals aren't interested and won't take them."

This, of course, is not the truth. Very seldom, in my experience, have I found a medical school or teaching hospital that had more bodies than it needed. In fact, just the opposite is generally true. They are actively seeking donations. You should be aware, however, that there are some things that will render a body less useful to science.

Schools usually want the full body in tact. This is the reason they usually won't take a body that has been autopsied. The schools also use the organs in their research. So, if the organs have been previously donated to organizations that focus on specific organs such as the eye bank, heart and lung bank, kidney bank, skin bank, etc, the school would lack the full body to work with and may decline. Generally, these institutions welcome any help along these lines that is offered.

Another nice thing about this option is that generally after one year, **they cremate the remains and return it to the family, free of charge.** As an option offering the opportunity to do a good act for science and humanity as well as minimize funeral expenses, donation to medical science is the ultimate. Total out-of-pocket expense to the family could be between $0 and $200 for some transportation charges to the school.

Memorial Societies

This is another source of information for keeping the costs of funeral down. There are some 120 Memorial Societies in the U.S. Membership fees start at $25 and up. Watch for the societies that may be affiliated with the funeral conglomerate. If you are in doubt, ask. Service Corporation International, (SCI) the largest corporate owner of funeral homes and cemeteries, in fact, owns the Neptune Society.

Memorial Societies are nonprofit, nonsectarian, educational organizations that helped increase the interest in cremation some 30 years ago. Volunteers mostly run these Societies. Memorial Societies are different from commercial businesses such as the Neptune Society of California, National Cremation Society of Florida, and Cremation and Memorial Society of Ohio, which are for-profit businesses. How do you know which are nonprofit organizations and which are the commercial societies? The real "societies" are nonprofit, educational organizations and are listed on the World Wide Web @ www.funerals.org/famsa, or call 802-482-3437, or write to FAMSA P.O. Box 10, Hinesburg, VT 05461.

5

Pros and Cons
for
Funeral Service Choices

The least expensive funeral today is direct or immediate cremation (or donation to science) with a memorial service at a church, meeting hall, golf club, or at home. This can cost as little as $450 in some parts of the United States.

If burial is preferred, a direct burial (which does not require embalming) followed by a memorial service is the next least expensive option. One should bear in mind the adage that funerals are actually for the living when considering what services and merchandise to purchase.

The most expensive funerals are arranged by and for people of modest means, while **the affluent tend towards modest ceremonies and cremation.** A good example of this is the cremation statistics in Marin County in San Francisco (which is a very affluent community) the cremation percentage of deaths in above 70% vs. the national average of 21%. Forty percent prefer cremation in California and Arizona.[1]

---

[1] *November, 1997, Harper's Magazine, Page 62*

There is an old saying, "You can't take it with you, but you can certainly leave as much of it as possible to your heirs and family". Conversely, I have seen many people of modest means who seem to think their life insurance or death benefits should be spent on one glorious event to mark their passing. The choice is yours as a personal preference, just be informed about your options.

The actual ceremony is up to you. Sometimes religious traditions dictate what you can or cannot do. Seek the advice of your minister, priest, rabbi, etc., and decide what is required and desired. Remember you can call it a funeral service or a memorial service as you choose. The standard difference being that memorial services are traditionally conducted without the body present, or having the body present in the form of cremains in an urn.

Direct Burial or Cremation?

As mentioned earlier, in some areas of the United States cremation has exceeded burial as the most common manner of handling the remains. In Marin County, California, for instance, about 70% choose cremation. In the Pacific Northwest about half the population requests cremation.[2] Cremations continue to increase every year. On a national average, 21 percent of all families choose cremation and there are several reasons why.[3]

First, we are a more mobile society these days, more prone to pack up our belongings and move to a pleasant climate, a better job, etc. With cremains, as the ashes of the deceased are known, you can pack up your deceased family members, too.

---

[2] *Cremation Association of North America www.funerals.org/famsa*
[3] *November, 1997, Harper's Magazine, Page 62*

From a purely economic standpoint, cremation will cost 50% to 80% less than burial, including memorial services. In most cities you can find a complete funeral with a metal casket for under $2,200 and cremation for under $550.[4]

Aesthetically, the ashes can be scattered in a favorite place or at sea, from an aircraft, or retained in an urn. Perhaps every bit as important as what you get with cremation is what you can do without.

Things you WON"T need if you elect cremation are:

➢ A casket. However, if you desire a viewing, most funeral homes have rental caskets for about $550 and up with changeable liners available for about $50 and UP....a savings of $500 to $10,000.

➢ A burial plot or mausoleum ($500 to $5,000, plus) unless you elect to have the ashes buried in a cemetery or placed in a niche.

➢ A vault/liner for the grave ($300 to $2,500 and UP). Some cemeteries require "Cremain Vaults". Believe it or not, this is a pure price gouge, since there's no real concern with the urn collapsing.

➢ A headstone ($450 and Up). For niches some form of plaque will be required, but this is generally less than a grave marker.

➢ The cost of opening and closing the grave ($300 to $800, or more)

➢ Pallbearers

➢ A hearse ($100 to $500) and/or limousines from chapel to graveside.

➢ Motorcycle escorts($75 to $150, or more)

For dispersal at-sea, from an aircraft, or on foreign soil, **Equitable Associates** can provide you a list of companies that perform this service, as well as U.S. Navy and Coast Guard Services for honorably discharged military personnel.

---

[4] *March 23, 1998, U.S. News & World Report, Page 56*

Advantages of Direct Burial or Cremation

This scenario, while gaining popularity with a public tired of inflated prices and prolonged ordeals, is not supported by the funeral industry for obvious reasons; it would cut funeral and burial costs by up to 60%!

Consider what would NOT be required in this case:

➤ Embalming

➤ Additional transportation fees (use of the hearse, utility vehicle or flower car, etc.)

➤ A funeral home and its staff and facilities charges

➤ Cosmetic and hair dressing charges

➤ Funeral chapel or church

➤ Viewing charges

➤ Common areas charges

➤ Parking lot fees

➤ Other fees and charges

Cemetery Choices, Ground Burial or Mausoleum

For burial you will need all the things mentioned above that are exclusions for cremation, starting with a burial plot.

Beware of cemetery salesman. They generally work on a commission-only basis". Funeral homes, which own or are directly affiliated with and participate in the profits of a cemetery, should be approached with care. If you are not sure of the cemetery's ownership, ask if they are affiliated with SCI, Loewen Group or Stewart Enterprises.

> Don't let your emotions cloud common sense when buying funeral merchandise and services.

Another way is to check your local newspaper classified ads for savings on cemetery lots. You'll find crypts and burial plots listed under **Cemetery Lots** or **Burial Lots** either by themselves or near the *Real Estate listings.* While the cost of these pre-purchased lots are usually very reasonable, some precautions are in order.

Be certain you check for outstanding balances at the cemetery concerned and that there isn't an exclusive clause stating the ownership is not transferable without the cemetery approval.

Church and religious-affiliated cemeteries often require their board of director's approval on any sale or transfer, *even among family members.* You'll want to make sure a marker permit is included, if required.

The cemetery would not issue a new deed until all outstanding balances have been settled. In any event, you also want to carefully read the deed or bill of sale. Plots are generally sold "**subject to current conditions and policies**", not necessarily what is stated on the bill of sale. It is the cemetery management that sets these conditions.

For instance, say you want to buy a plot that was last sold in 1980. In 1980 each grave was sold with the condition that for each burial the grave would be opened and closed for a sum of $100. The current policy states $400. You will be required to pay $400...not what is stated on the 1980 document. Before purchasing, be sure to check with the cemetery for current <u>policies and conditions</u> to know what you are actually getting.

Cemetery rules and regulations are kind of like Covenants, Conditions & Restrictions in a subdivision.

Your funeral director likely keeps the phone numbers and the basic price information about all the cemeteries in the area and can provide you with guidance in this direction. This list can serve as a good starting point for comparing prices. It's probably much easier to get information over the telephone than in person, and save some of the high-pressure sales ploys. You could also try to contact several cemeteries in your area. Or, you could call **Equitable Associates,** and we can help you in getting better prices from a broker if there is one or more in your area.

As a rule the funeral director does NOT receive a commission for any sales he steers to the cemetery. This is not the case where the funeral home and cemetery are under the same roof, or corporately owned, as is the case with Stewart Enterprises, Loewen Group or SCI-affiliated/owned funeral homes and cemeteries.

You Can Do Both…Cremation AND Burial

There's no rule, which says you can't have both burial and cremation. Many people elect cremation and have their ashes interred in the cemetery with their family. There's a complete line of products for this purpose and, yes, some cemeteries have anticipated this by requiring the use of a **cremains vault!** If this is still the cemetery of your choice, there is not a way around this issue unless you choose another method of disposition of the cremains within the cemetery. Perhaps you might choose the cemetery rose garden, the columbarium, or select another cemetery.

The human body yields about 6 to 10 pounds of ashes and/or ground bone fragments after cremation. The cemetery will sell you whatever you are willing to spend. A nice covered vase or humidor (cigar box) will work very nicely as a way to reduce costs.

Mausoleums: Possibly A Better Value!

While we're here, let's consider the cost of mausoleums. We've all seen them in old movies and perhaps at the more posh memorial parks and, likely as not, figured they were reserved for the particularly well to do. Perhaps not, considering the total outlay of the alternative ground burial.

Mausoleum crypts sell for around $1,000 per space and up. As is the case with cremation, the true value lies in what you **won't** have to pay for:

➢ No opening/closing of the grave ($375 to $1,050), although there will likely be " sealing"," encrypting charge" or similar charge.
➢ No Vault/Liner ($400, plus).
➢ No Marker/Monument ($500, plus) and, again, there will be some similar marker, though generally much less expensive).
➢ No Burial Plot ($400, plus).

All things considered, mausoleums are probably a good buy. This is particularly true in the case of those (the deceased or family) who have an aversion to the ground burial. Mausoleums allow visitation in all weather conditions and some offer a chapel and/or a visiting lounge in the atrium, which is temperature-controlled and pleasant. With mausoleum industry giants like Gibraltar (now owned by SCI) are leading the way with pre-sold units built as demand dictates, look for them to increase in popularity, particularly since the cost of a routine ground burial is already as much or more than a crypt in a mausoleum.

Most state laws say that you can sell mausoleum crypts on a "pre-need" basis, and the law also says that construction wouldn't have to begin for up to eight years after its capacity has been sold out. Think about it…what would happen if you died tomorrow and you are holding a piece of ownership paper for the construction of your crypt at a future date and there is no crypt ready for you now?

Know what you are getting; go see it, and don't be overly trusting until you see it built. Make sure your crypt is physically built before you purchase it. You never know when you will need it.

Loopholes Allowed By The FTC
Under The Funeral Rule Of 1984

Webster describes a loophole, as "a means of escape: an ambiguity or omission in the text through which the intent of a statute, contract, or obligation may be evaded."

Here's a loophole for you. Yes, a 1994 directive from the FTC—again in conflict with the original rule—indicates that the price of cremation does not need to be included in the price for an immediate or direct cremation if the funeral home doesn't own the crematory. Such cost would then be considered a "cash advance" item. How can one have an immediate/direct cremation without cremation? Confusing to consumers who wouldn't think to ask if cremation were included? You bet! Even when the same people own the crematory and funeral home, there may be a different corporation running each. So you'd better ask what the total price will be *including cremation,* if that's your choice. Otherwise, there may be an unexpected $200to $300 charge added to your total cost.

A 1994 amendment to the FTC's Funeral Rule now allows funeral homes to add **all** overhead to a non-declinable basic charge for planning the funeral, a fee that should be less than $400. with no limits on this fee, it has effectively become a guaranteed income for the funeral directors, a situation that invites consumer abuse, especially in areas where there are far more funeral homes than can supported by the death rate. In just two years, this fee has risen to $1000 of $1700 or more at many funeral homes, with all other costs such as the casket and funeral service being added to that.

Some funeral homes have justified the size of this fee by saying that this fee includes: "Compliance with infectious waste management regulations and employee safety regulations mandated by governmental agencies." To which Jessica Mitford has a delightful retort: "Imagine that! They're going to charge you for not breaking the law."

When the non-declinable fee is grossly inflated, it limits the options of a price-sensitive consumer. Furthermore, someone selecting a simple graveside service uses far less of the funeral home's overhead, yet will be paying to maintain portions of a fancy establishment that won't be needed. This is in direct conflict with the intent of the original Funeral Rule.

Although consumers groups pressed the FTC to include cemeteries under the provision of the Funeral Rule, this was not done. Consequently the portion of your funeral arrangement that involves a cemetery may be loaded with pitfalls.

Information FAMSA web site.

6

What You Need to Know About Funeral Homes & Cemeteries

The Funeral Home

Selecting a funeral home should be done prior to having the body moved.

The initial criteria for selecting a funeral home will likely be a mixture of tradition, reputation, and research. Few funeral homes are new in business, as most of them have been doing business for generations. So, finding someone with experience shouldn't be hard.

As a rule, funeral homes are local concerns, marketing to a specific area; many count on the community's loyalty to the exclusion of competitive pricing. Call around outside your neighborhood. I have found in the majority of cases that the more extensive the façade and the more numerous the staff, the higher the charges will likely be to cover that excess overhead.

Call and request their General Price List on services. You may also request prices of funeral merchandise, caskets, vaults or cremains urns. Some may refuse to give you a casket and merchandise price list as the law only requires them to furnish you with the General Price List.

With regard to cremain urns, these little ornate boxes and vases for storing ashes can run into the HUNDREDS OF DOLLARS! Sometimes the salesperson will tell you that this urn is not large enough to hold your loved ones ashes. Just know that you can provide your own container, be it a Tupperware bowl, or a rare Ming vase, so don't be swayed by a fancy sales pitches.

The cremains are merely pulverized remains of the more solid bone fragments, a substance somewhere between sand and small pieces of gravel in consistency. I have seen cigar humidors used to hold the ashes, they look very similar to the solid mahogany boxes sold as a cremains urn for over $600. Use your imagination and, while you're looking, have the cremains stored in a minimal container, which is a plastic box that is sometimes provided by the crematory as part of the cremation fee. If this is not provided as part of the cremation fee the crematory may charge $10-$25 for this minimal plastic container.

The funeral is a *social event,* and the disposition of the remains is a personal decision. This is why getting the person's desires beforehand is vital, both for his or her satisfaction and your peace of mind.

Once you have the price information in hand, make a tour of the various funeral homes. Expect some pressure

> *An old time funeral director told me many years ago, "If you want to see if the funeral homes really cares about families, check the toilet paper in the restrooms. If it's plush they care □ if it's cheap industrial single-ply, move on. they're more interested in profits than service."*

to put your name on a dotted line or to verbally agree to contract for services. Resist! And, be sure to take your friend along to be the dissenting voice, should you need one. If the person that you are making arrangements for is still alive and has to be consulted in the decision-making process, a good *"out"* should you encounter pressure; *"I'll need to talk with my uncle to see what he prefers."*

Watch what you wear when visiting these funeral homes. The funeral director and his sales force are very good at summing up potential at a glance. If you arrive wearing your Rolex and lots of jewelry, you can bet you won't be shown anything but top–of-the -line caskets, vaults, and other service packages. Bear in mind that all the mood lighting, velvet drapes, soft carpets, and smooth voices are designed to create an atmosphere of profound respectability….*and* it comes at a price. Just be aware that those who pay $700 for a respectable casket will get the same atmosphere as those who mortgage their futures for a swank bronze casket.

Check for such things as parking, lounge areas, cleanliness and attitude of the staff you encounter. If they yank you in off the porch, you might want to look elsewhere. Most will be considerate and admire your taking the initiative to plan ahead. Some may even suggest ways of holding expenses down, if you ask. Not all funeral homes are out to get you, they all are, however, in business to make money. You are just looking for equitable pricing.

Tell the funeral home, up front, that you have discussed the required services with your mother, father, aunt or uncle or whoever and that your needs will be specific, right down to the make and model of the vault. This lets them know you'll not be easily swayed or led along more expensive paths and that you have at least a nodding acquaintance with the funeral business. If nothing else, **Equitable Associates'** information should give you a familiarity with the terminology used in the funeral industry, and that should set you apart from the usual customer.

An old time funeral director told me this many years ago, "If you want to see if the funeral homes really cares about families, check the toilet paper in the restrooms. If it's plush they care, if it's cheap industrial single-ply, move on. They're more interested in profits than service."

Funeral Home Prices

Funeral Homes break down their prices under four broad headings;

➤ **Professional Services:**

> **May** include a few basic services, but is usually used to cover overhead and profit, providing NOTHING in return for your money.

➤ **Use of Facilities and Staff:**

> **May** include the use of chapel for viewing as part of the funeral ceremony, or the memorial service. Also includes graveside services.

➤ **Transportation:**

> **May** include transfer of deceased via hearse, limousine, other automotive equipment, flower car, etc. and additional mileage charges outside a fixed range.

➤ **Prices for Merchandise Selected:**

> Casket or alternative burial container, vault or liner, cremation urn, clothing, and other merchandise.

There is a fifth heading called **Cash Advance, which covers all the goods** and services the funeral director must pay out of pocket to third parties on your behalf. Be careful that no extra fee is charged for their advancing cash on your behalf. Federal regulation prohibits the funeral director from profiting from these expenses without disclosing that fact to the consumer. [5]

Usually included under cash advance items are:

Honorarium for clergy	Flowers
Newspaper Notice (obituary)	Organist
Soloist	Death Certificates (per copy)

---

[5] *April 30, 1984, Funeral Rule, Section 453.3 Misrepresentation (f)*

Other Funeral Home Charges (police escort, parking lot help, etc)

Air Transportation   Permits

Crematory Charge   Sales Taxes

Other Misc. Charges

It is customary for these items to be on a separate summary sheet. Looking over the list you will likely find several items you would prefer to handle yourself such as asking a friend to sing for you. Funeral directors would be pleased if you do since these items represent immediate cash paid out by the funeral home. Still it's nice to know these things are available, particularly if you've ever tried to locate someone to sing a favorite song on short notice.

Embalming

Misleading information by the funeral industry has lead people to believe that embalming was a legal requirement when direct cremation or direct burial was the choice of disposition.

Embalming may be required under the following conditions:

➢ When death occurs from some infectious diseases.
➢ Where the disposition cannot take place in the required time set by each state; i.e. 24 to 48 hours.
➢ Where there is a public viewing or traditional funeral service with the body present.
➢ Where the body is shipped in a common carrier such as a train, airplane or ship.

Practicality may dictate the need for embalming; the law does not. When the law does require embalming, it is seldom for public safety reasons but more to minimize the unpleasant odor of an unembalmed body awaiting burial or cremation.

Refrigeration, however, may meet the family's need for a short viewing period or a closed casket service. Ask the funeral director about the use of refrigeration in lieu of embalming in your case. Sometimes funeral directors may waive the refrigeration charges. Why not ask?

Many sales personnel know only what they are told by their superiors. They are sincere in what they say and tend to quote specific figures for comparison when asked. Each case is different and should be priced according to its own merits and not from a canned presentation. Don't buy a service package because someone says, "That includes the embalming, which is required by law" since this may not be totally true

An example, a study by NFDA (National Funeral Directors Association) cited the casket as composing only 14% of the cost of an "average funeral" when in reality it was more than 50% the cost. Some sales personnel are trained to say that burial vaults **were required**, due to legislation on environmental issues, specifically rainwater run off, etc.[6] This is creative selling, and I have not found this to be the truth anywhere. <u>Just remember that even if the salesperson is sincere and telling what he or she knows to be the truth, you may be the one paying for his or her unawareness of the facts.</u>

Opening and Closing the Grave

This is one service it pays to know a bit about. Charges vary across the United States. In fact, some grave openings/closings are included in the price of the plot, though some maintain this service only accrues to the original purchaser. **Fees can vary widely according to the day of the week or even the time of day that the opening or closing is performed.**

An example is a cemetery that charges $500 to open and close (dig the grave and fill it in) a grave during the week, prior to 3:30 p.m. If this is done at a later time, the charge could go up approximately $100 more. Saturday before 1 p.m., $650. After 1 p.m. on Saturday, it goes to $750, and for any time on Sunday or holidays, the charge is (can you

---

[6] *www.nfda.org/resources/funeral*

believe this?) $1,050! Knowing this in advance could save you several hundreds of dollars.

Again, the only way to know for certain is to ask. You should also be aware that some of the larger burial vault companies, such as Wilbert, "set their vaults into the grave for free. More than a few families have been charged for the setting of a Wilbert vault by the cemetery when they should not have been charged at all.

What You Should Know About Vaults and Grave Liners

These items are becoming required in many, if not most cemeteries. They are concrete shells into which the casket is lowered. The rationale behind them (depending upon which salesman you talk to) is to keep moisture out of the casket and to keep the surface of the grave from collapsing once the casket deteriorates. Another is to prevent the weight of the dirt from crushing the casket (an unlikely immediate event, but a good sales ploy).

What they actually provide is a nice, level surface for ease of mowing and a solid profit center for the cemetery. As with caskets, it is illegal for them to tout the protective merits of a burial vault. It is ludicrous to do so, in fact, considering many have holes in their bottoms to prevent the whole thing from floating up. They will delay the casket collapse, however.

Tree roots can penetrate at-will and, according to numerous sources within the industry, if you want a vault that is truly waterproof, you'll need to spend thousands of dollars, perhaps as much as $10,000. Here we're talking the deluxe, seamless bronze vaults, and even these are not impervious to roots.

<u>Vaults</u>

Vaults usually portray security and, as such, cost more. A vault is simply a completely enclosed two-piece box with a sealing lid made of reinforced concrete, sometimes coated with asphalt mix. Sometimes the vault is concrete lined with metal, fiberglass or plastic. Vaults can also be made of steel, either galvanized or non-galvanized from 10 to 12 gauge thickness.

Liners

These are sometimes referred to as rough box and it is a four-sided reinforced concrete box with no bottom and a loose fitting lid. This is lowered into the ground before the graveside service. These are usually less expensive than vaults and serve the same purpose. Either one or the other can be purchased for the gravesite, not both.

The interesting thing about vaults and liners is
that we have our clergymen quote that old adage
"ashes to ashes and dust to dust", and
then we go to extreme lengths and expense
to keep that from happening!

Nature won't allow this, of course, and given time we'll all return to our elements no matter how much we spend on funeral merchandise. This is another example of funeral merchandise sales gimmicks.

Knowing the language can, once again, save you money. Price a vault, then price a grave liner. Vaults and liners accomplish (or fail to accomplish) the same things, and yet the price of the vault may be several times more that of a liner! Funeral sales training said this was because the word *vault* just sounds more substantial than *liner*. So, ask for a liner, if one is required. It will cost you less.

Monuments

Refer to the information on *How To Select A Monument*. Okay, you've located the cemetery you want and, even if you haven't finalized the purchase of a plot, you need to look ahead to the other things that need to be considered. While touring the cemeteries did you look at the monuments? Did you take some notes and measurements? Now its time to visit some monument companies. Ask a lot of questions while you're there and, just as in the case of caskets, realize that the stones on display represent only a small portion of what's actually available.

Some of the more advanced monuments companies now have software that can display color graphics of what any stone will look like with your information on it. This keeps you from being surprised or disappointed later and will help you *balance* the information and make a wiser choice. Get several quotes and, if possible, a color printout or sales brochure of the stones that would most likely to appeal to the decision maker. If the deceased had some input prior to death, include that input as well, and if this was a pre-arranged purchase by the deceased by all means use that choice.

One other caution, the monument is sometimes sold in two pieces, the engraved headstone and a granite base for it to set upon. Make certain you price BOTH pieces! In some cases the headstone is sold at a reasonable price only to have the matching base marked-up more than double.

Basic Consumer Advice

♦ Know how much a funeral service should cost.

♦ Choose a funeral home with reasonable price –regardless of its location in the metro area.

♦ Avoid harmful "protective sealer" caskets; choose a less costly non-sealing metal casket.

♦ Be cautious about Pre-Pay Plans. Most "lock-in" high prices; and /or are non-refundable, non-cancelable. Open your own "Totten Trust" or "POD-Account" (Payable-on-Demand account).

♦ Don't assign entire funeral policy to a funeral home, but only the amount you need to spend.

♦ Changing Funeral homes. If the body is at an unfairly priced funeral home—even if the funeral home has done some work on the body—you have the right to change to another funeral home. Call an equitable priced funeral home to obtain the body. You don't need to talk to the first funeral home again.

♦ Consider purchasing your casket from a dealer or wholesaler, or call Equitable Associates, or make your own.

♦ Buy an inexpensive basic casket, and personalize with pillow/bedding from home. Personalize the funeral any way you wish (as weddings and other celebrations); you don't need the funeral directors permission. Cooperative equitable priced funeral homes offer decorative hardware, symbols, religious pictures you can put in the casket lid; use art from stores or family photos; let children help with poems, art, streamers, balloons, flowers from home.

♦ Find a funeral home that will let you do what you want to honor your loved one.

7

How to Select a Casket

If you decide to have the body viewed in a casket, with delayed burial (or cremation), you need to phone several funeral homes and request a copy of their **General Price List, Casket List,** and their **Credit Policy.** Tell them you can pick them up or ask them mail these to you, if they will.

If you get prices quoted over the telephone, without actually reading the fine print, you'll have no idea what you are really buying at those prices. Federal law now requires funeral homes to provide the General Price List to anyone requesting it, **however, they <u>are not</u> required to furnish you with a copy of the casket prices that you can take home.** Some will be obliging and some will not.

Since 1984 the Federal Trade Commission (FTC) instituted the **Funeral Rule** which mandates that caskets are NOT REQUIRED for cremations without viewing, and that all customers are to be given a detailed price list for services (even over the phone!). Also required is to show a complete price list of caskets and other related merchandise. *(For a copy of the Funeral Rule, call Equitable Associates and we will send you a copy.)*

Know in advance that they would rather have a "Grief Counselor" go over the prices with you, *to help explain your options.* Despite all that sympathy and understanding, know that their paycheck depends upon them *helping you* make choices that will fatten their bank accounts.

If you pick up the General Price List in person, dress casually. What you will pay is often determined by what the funeral director THINKS you can afford, according to your clothes, jewelry, the automobile you are driving, and you will be persuasively steered in that direction.

If you have dealt with the funeral home before you may expect to hear about your belated relative who had the most upscale funeral. They were likely going over your family file shortly before you arrived. Be careful about what financial information you divulge, and be tight-lipped about specific amounts of life insurance, and other such benefits.

> *Be careful about what you reveal about your personal finances!*

> *A lady whose husband had just died arrived at a funeral home bearing all of her husband's papers related to his death, including a life insurance policy with the benefit of $10,000. Once finished with the Grief Counselor, she walked away with a $10,000 funeral service.*

While at the funeral home, ask to see their casket display room. Once in the display room, **DON'T FALL FOR THE...**"These are the only models we stock or are available", *or* "anything else will be a special order and may take a while to get here" gimmick.

Most funeral homes stock only fifteen or so models due to space considerations. There are hundreds of models and colors available to choose from. If you select one from the floor, odds are the actual casket will be delivered from a regional warehouse, the same as any "special order" you might select, which is generally available within a few hours anywhere in the country.

Jot down the makes and models numbers that appeal to you, along with preferred colors and linings. Pay special attention to **gauge** numbers (often listed as 18# or 20#) in the case of steel caskets, or **weight** in the case of bronze and copper (e.g., 34 oz, etc.). You can shop these by phone later and **save yourself about 50%.**

A COMMON PLOY:

You would want only <u>the best</u> for your loved one, wouldn't you?

This is the most common sales gimmick that is played even at the best-respected community funeral homes. This ploy is based upon the marketing principle that **no one wants to look cheap** where a loved one is involved. They also recognize that **you cannot buy what they can't see!**

The funeral home, almost always, will show you the top of the line first (a mahogany or bronze model, depending on how you are dressed and the model car you drive). These models cost several thousand dollars. Next, they'll show you their "Economy Line", which is to say a less attractive model in steel which is still quite expensive. Finally, they'll show you the model *they* want you to buy, possibly a 16-gauge steel model. It will be a few hundred dollars more than the least expensive model, but thousands less than the top of the line.

The thing you need to remember: **THE MODELS THEY SHOW YOU COULD BE MORE THAN YOU WANT TO SPEND!** *The average mark-up over their entire cost is likely 400-700%.*

There are several hundred models of perfectly lovely caskets readily available in the $700-$1,400 range. Be prepared before you arrive with a dollar figure in mind and demand that you be shown models in that range, along with the color and lining options available for each.

> *Over the years I have repeatedly seen a flip chart used to*
> *show various casket materials and the advantages of each.*
> *Fancy mahogany and bronze were at the top,*
> *copper and oak in the middle, and steel and*
> *poplar as the low end on each page.*

> <u>*The true low-cost pine and cloth covered*</u>
> <u>*pressed-board were not even listed.*</u>

> *If you chose the "middle range" on the flip chart*
> *(Copper or Oak) it would likely cost you*
> *200-400% more than a true medium price steel*
> *casket with no additional benefits.*

ANOTHER COMMON PLOY:

"It Only Comes In Gray."

Most funeral homes do have reasonably priced models. And, if you insist, don't be surprised if you are taken to the backroom, garage, basement, or in a dark hallway to see these displayed in unflattering colors such as gray. Again, this is a gimmick and they are playing with your emotions.

Be aware that you can purchase these "gray" models from the warehouse in several colors and linings. Therefore, demand it.

HERE'S ANOTHER GIMMICK:

"We Have Nothing in Your Price Range".

You will often hear the old saying, **"We don't have anything in your price range in a PROTECTIVE casket"**. The idea of a *protective seal* to keep out dirt, water, roots, etc. is preposterous! It is also **illegal for any claims of protection to be made!**

In fact, a seal is detrimental to the remains in that it promotes growth of anaerobic bacteria in the body cavity which produces gases that bloat the remains to the point that some literally explode. This is why mausoleums require *the seals on caskets be broken or removed* prior to placing the casket in their compartments.

This <u>protective seal scam </u>is pure salesmanship. If they can get you to envision your loved one in that lovely casket, even though they are dead, certainly you wouldn't want water

---

PRINCIPLE #4:   A seal is important to auto transmissions and canned goods, NOT to corpses.

---

or moisture to get in and being air tight you might rationalize that it would preserve the body as you remembered it.

Why are the consumers paying extra for something that *sounds good*, but is in fact harmful or useless?

It is because a salesman's paycheck is dependent upon a percentage of what he sells each month. Incidentally, the funeral director pays about $12.00 for the rubber gasket (seal), then charges you as much as $500.

Okay, you've visited and collected your lists. Take the price lists to a neutral site. Some place other than the funeral home; perhaps a restaurant or coffee shop. Your home may not be advisable, especially if the terminally ill person is at your home. Have an emotionally stable friend meet you. Study these price lists and *read the fine print.* Learn what's available in terms of service and what each will cost.

There will likely be a range of packages offered some with names like Earth Burial Package #1, etc. Study these closely since there will likely be things included you don't want or need and others not listed that you may want or need.

> **DO NOT BUY,**
> **OR**
> **AGREE TO BUY,**
> **A CASKET**
> **AT THIS TIME!**

From the General Price List you can price services individually against those included in packages. You may then make your own offer for a custom package that may work much better in terms of both satisfaction and cost.

Be aware of ancillary or additional charges such as the use of the funeral home parking lot. This could be an extra $100 or more per day. Also for use of the chapel for viewing periods which may be three or four-hour segments amounting to several periods per day and charged by the period. Often $150 or more is charged for each four-hour period. Also, look for additional charges for **common areas,** which include lounges, the kitchen, and restrooms.

You may not want to use the lounge and you might want to say that if you didn't use the lounge, what kind of deduction would there be?

WARNING! Be aware of packages that are based on the number of Memorial Events! Viewing periods, memorial services, funeral services, transfers to church or gravesite, and who-knows-what-else constitutes an event. This could be a way of generating additional charges. Should you want an extra event, say perhaps three viewing periods plus an extra memorial service when the package only covers three memorial events, be aware that you will pay extra. Extra events are expensive, so, as an alternative you may want to price the services from the General Price List. You may even be able to trade a hearse for a viewing period, etc.

WARNING! Be aware that what you <u>call or name</u> the service may sometimes determine the price. As an example, rental of the funeral home chapel for a **memorial service** may well go for $260, while rental of the funeral home chapel for a **funeral service** may go for $460. There is no set definition of either. Typically, if the body is present it's called a funeral service. However, if the body is absent or in the form of cremains, it's called a memorial service. **If any service price is not specified, ask and get it in writing.** As an example, a service in a park or at the local golf club or down by the seashore, etc.

WARNING! Pay particular attention to any package that suggests the prices are only valid if you purchase a casket from the funeral home. This may be a ploy to imply you must buy a casket from them in order to get that package price. **THIS IS ILLEGAL!** Also illegal is for the funeral home to charge a **"Casket Handling Fee"** for caskets that are purchased elsewhere and delivered to their funeral home.

You can generally buy the casket and/or burial vault from another source at a better price. A common ploy, and one that was recommended in a national funeral industry magazine, is to request that a family member be present to *inspect* the casket when it is delivered.[7] They cannot require you to be present *and,* it is unprofessional. Unfortunately, it happens. Most people want to get the details over with and get out of there. If an obstacle such an inconvenience is presented to the family where they have to come back, they might surrender and allow the funeral home to order the casket in order not to deal with any more emotional stress.

Many funeral homes are family owned and are therefore more flexible in their terms. They would likely forego an extra $500 to $1000 of additional profit on a casket rather than lose $2,500 worth of services. **So speak up if you think the casket or burial vault is priced too high.**

Most often when a family calls for a price comparison, the family-owned funeral home usually gives the family the casket at a lower price rather than lose all the family's goodwill.

> ## Everything is Negotiable!

Be aware that big conglomerates like SCI (Service Corporation International), Stewart Enterprises, and Loewen Group. These corporations own about a quarter of all the funeral homes and cemeteries in the United States. These funeral homes have their prices and policies pretty much dictated from their corporate headquarters. This means far less flexibility in pricing, as a rule.

Ask on your initial phone call, if SCI, Stewart Enterprises, or Loewen Group owns the funeral home then factor this into your decision when selecting a funeral home to serve you. This, too, **could save you 40-50% since some of these conglomerates report profits per funeral FOUR TIMES HIGHER than an independently owned funeral home.**[8]

SCI continues to buy out more of the competition. Their most recent acquisition is the mausoleum giant, Gibraltar, and a small funeral chain called Affordable Funerals.[9]

---

[7] *Interfaith Funeral Information Committee - www.xroads.com/~funerals*
[8] *National Funeral Directors Association, and SEC figures for 1996*
[9] *Interfaith Funeral Information Committee – www.xroads.com/~funerals*

Father Henry Wasielewski, a Catholic Priest, has dedicated much of the past three decades to revealing the excesses of the funeral industry. His market surveys reveal **SCI's prices average about 35% more than other funeral homes across the nation.** [10] The other conglomerate funeral homes are similar.

Additional Information about Caskets

According to the annual price survey conducted by the National Funeral Directors Association (NFDA), the funeral industry's trade group, the typical American adult funeral cost $4,783 in 1997. Cemetery expenses such as gravesite, interment and marker can bring the total to $8,000 or so. In the past five years, the price of dying has risen about three times faster than the consumer's price index. CASKETS MAKE UP NEARLY HALF THE COST OF THE AVERAGE FUNERAL, according to NFDA figures. The cheapest are so-called alternative containers; usually cloth covered wood or cardboard, selling for between $35 and $465. At the other extreme are those made of what funeral directors call semi-precious metal — bronze and copper![11]

More than any other facet of the funeral business, the casket is routinely subject to outrageous price inflation on behalf of the funeral homes by outrageous mark-ups of 500% and more with the national average falling somewhere around 400%. [12]

Caskets and vaults are actually quite reasonable if purchased from manufacturers, and there are a few funeral homes and a few "casket stores" out there that can meet your needs at a reasonable price. You just cannot always count on your funeral home to provide you with an **EQUITABLE PRICE.** Reasonable Retail prices would be 1.5 to 2.0 times wholesale, Lowest Retail price in the U.S. is 1.5 times wholesale. Most Common Retail price is 2.5 to 5.0 times wholesale.[13]

---

[10] *Interfaith Funeral Information Committee.- www.xroads.com/~funerals*
[11] *September, 1997, Money Magazine, Pages 88 and 89*
[12] *March, 1998, U.S. News & World Report, Page 52*
[13] *Interfaith Funeral Information Committee: www.xroads.com/~funerals.*

WARNING! Be aware of word games. Anytime you mention selecting a more reasonable casket, you may hear the funeral industry's use of the words: **disposal of the remains** of your loved one, as in, *This wood composite box would be adequate for the disposal of the remains, but we can't guarantee anything about it.*[14] **(These words are used to play on your emotions and to evoke in you a feeling of heartlessness.)**

The forces of nature can be delayed for a time,

but cannot be stopped!

Are you willing to pay extra for this time?

Burial, cremation, donation, whatever you want to call it, actually **is** the disposal of the remains. They know, and you should know also, that *disposal* sounds far more heartless than the word *disposition* of the remains. **Don't get taken to the cleaners over semantics.** Word games are big in funeral home marketing schemes.

Speaking the Casket Language

Steel caskets are listed by **gauge,** which is to say the thickness of the steel used; with the lower the gauge number the thicker the steel. You'll see 16 gauge, 18 gauge, 19 gauge, 20 gauge commonly listed. The difference between top-of-line and average is like the difference between the thickness of a stop sign and the thickness of a car fender. **You will be encouraged to go for the lower gauge for its increased security.** This is impractical or misleading for this reason.

The casket itself will likely be enclosed in a vault of concrete or metal, which lines the gravesite. (Cemeteries maintain this is for added protection, but it is really for the cosmetics of the cemetery and for easy maintenance to keep the ground level). Hence,

---

[14] *Interfaith Funeral Information Committee: www.xroads.com/~funerals*

an extra sale for the cemetery or funeral home when the lower gauge is clearly not needed.

Steel caskets start around $400 for a 20-gauge model with crepe lining. The national average price is closer to $1,200 for the 20-gauge.[15] They are the most popular of all the caskets and, as such, often have a hefty mark-up, which puts them at the "for a few dollars more you can have the copper or mahogany" level. **Bait and Switch is a popular ploy** throughout the industry, so watch for it when the initial prices are low.

Copper and bronze are the casket elite, starting at about $3,500 and progressing rapidly to $10,000 and more. The absolute top of the line can run you $20,000, or more, depending on what part of the country you live in and how gullible you are.

Copper and bronze caskets are listed in weight categories, such as 32-ounce and 48-ounce, representing the ounces per square foot of material. The key selling points of these caskets are that they don't rust and they're the top-of-the-line — **(snob appeal).**

You may also be told they offer superior protection, better seals, and other things. They don't. The tighter the seal the less *natural* the decomposition. The seals are basically the same and the mechanism to seal the casket is the same, but because copper and bronze is impervious to rust, it is alleged that it offers better protection as opposed to steel.

Wooden caskets are made of mahogany, walnut, cherry, oak, maple, or poplar. There are also some nice models made of pine, but you're not likely to see them, or know of their existence at all unless you specifically ask.

Wood models run from about $2,000 for poplar to $4,000 and up for mahogany. Pine can start around $300, and even the least expensive model can be draped with a flag or augmented with floral arrangements to good advantage.

---

[15] *Interfaith Information Committee www.xroads.com/~funerals*

Figure about $300 to $1,500 for a nice wooden or metal casket and let the funeral director find you the options in this range. If the funeral director cannot, call **Equitable Associates'** **toll free pager number: 1-888-556-1350.** We can find some nice wooden and metal caskets that are quite reasonable and readily available to ship to your funeral home.

Wooden caskets are beautiful works of art and are suitable to the individual who would appreciate fine furniture. They are perfectly suitable for burial using the standard concrete liner, however, you may be persuaded to spend extra money to purchase a vault lined with copper or fiberglass. The funeral director's sales pitch will allege this gives extra protection from the elements.

Most cemeteries require some type of concrete liners for the grave which will average somewhere between $255 to $340 or optional concrete vaults which are two-piece concrete boxes usually sprayed with a asphalt material on the outside and painted either gold or silver. These could run you in the neighborhood of $450 to $600.

If you opt for a lower end casket expect a strong sales pitch for more expensive burial vaults. These too, are subject to horrendous mark-ups and, despite all the claims of protection, many models have holes in the bottom.

Something new in the marketplace in the way of a wooden casket is called a **Madeiron,** which is a simulated wood made from nutshells. Currently these are offered for sale in Spain, but may be coming to the U.S. before long due to their reasonable cost (less than $150), biodegradability, and stylish appearance. Madeiron can be shaped and stained to look identical to the $8,000 mahogany model, yet costs less than a rental casket.

This casket would be an ideal option for an open-casket service followed by cremation or donation but, as you might imagine, neither the casket manufacturers nor the funeral homes are anxious to see them imported. The cost-effectiveness of this material could change the wooden casket market, as we know it.

Rental caskets have been around since the early 1970's. It is a casket with no bottom that slips over an alternative container. These are primarily used with cremations where people want a nicer casket for a service but do not want to buy a casket only to have it burned up. After the service, the deceased is already in the alternative container ready to go to the crematory. These are losing favor because funeral homes have priced the rental rates so high.

If you choose to have an immediate or direct cremation, the funeral director will offer you either an inexpensive alternative container or an unfinished wood box. An alternative container is a non-metal enclosure used to hold the deceased. These containers may be made of pressboard, cardboard, or canvas. Because any container you buy will be destroyed during the cremation, you may wish to use an alternative container or an unfinished wood box. These could lower your funeral cost since they are less expensive than burial caskets. Under the Federal Rule, funeral directors who offer direct cremation must disclose in writing your right to buy an unfinished wood box (which is a type of casket) or an alternative container. They must make an unfinished wood box or alternative container available for immediate or direct cremation purposes.[16]

I mentioned earlier that you should list the model number, color, lining, hardware options, etc., in order to "shop" the cost of the casket. **Equitable Associates** has a list of reasonable casket providers who stock most brands and can deliver virtually any of them within hours to the funeral home of your choice. Find the model and color you like, check the prices available in your locality, then call **Equitable Associates' toll free pager number 1-888-556-1350** to get an alternate source for the same or similar product.

---

[16]*Funeral Rule, Section 453.3, Misrepresentations, (b) (1) and Section 453.1, Definitions (a)*

All of our recommendations are without commission. We put you in contact with each vendor or funeral home. You make your own financial arrangements with them.

The average cost to the family is approximately $200 over wholesale. As a general rule, this includes delivery to the funeral home within a few hours. This alone could cut the cost of the funeral by hundreds while still providing everything you want.

Okay, by now you should have enough information to have the body delivered to the funeral home of your choice. Now you need to consider whether you will have a service. And if so, whether it will be a funeral service with a viewing or a memorial service without the body present. Next you need to decide where these will ultimately take place.

Your next step is to choose a final disposition. You have several alternatives. Refer back to "Overview of Choices for Funerals".

8

How To Select A Monument

A Lasting Tribute for All to See

You can spend as much or as little as you want on monuments, headstones, markers, memorials, etc. The median price falls around $800 nationwide and it is customary to wait until things have leveled off to a less emotional state before ordering one.

A common remark from families who have arranged funerals over the years was that they wished they had spent **more on the monument** and **less on the casket.**

For this reason some extra care should be exercised in selecting the monument.

Some cemeteries require a particular type of stone or bronze plaque and, (no surprise here) provide them at a set cost or make them a part of the burial plot sales package. This is another thing to consider when selecting a burial plot, and a hurdle in getting a better price at some other cemetery if this is the only cemetery in town.

Monuments come in about three forms, the standard gray granite, colored granite and marble, or a bronze plaque placed flat on the ground (usually mounted to a concrete base). Buyers over age 60 tend to buy traditional gray granite, while buyers in their 50's or younger choose colored granite or marble. Bronze is something few elect of their own accord, but is often required by the cemetery association for easy maintenance (by being able to mow over these flush-mounted plaques) without chipping or damage problems from lawn maintenance equipment. This is also another way to pad their pockets. So, shop for cemeteries that can provide you with your preferences…not theirs.

Important To Note: **Unlike all other funeral expenses, a monument is a lasting tribute for all to see.**

Granite is preferable to marble, in most instances, because marble tends to oxidize and wear away or discolor more readily than the harder granite. Granite comes in three grades; Light (which is the least expensive but is most likely to show pollution or stains), Medium (a good grade), and Dark (the most dense and stable). Know which grade you're getting and take that into account when considering price. The mere fact that you are aware that there are multiple grades will make you less likely to be taken, so please ask.

Where you buy your monument in the U.S. will also play a part in its price. South of the Mason-Dixon Line, most stone is Georgia Granite. North, the stone will likely be Barre Granite from Barre, Vermont. What's the difference in quality? None. The difference is Price? Maybe as much as 50% due to Vermont companies having to pay union wages and higher shipping costs.

Being the informed shopper that you are by now, tell the monument company or cemetery that you want your marker to be made from Georgia Granite, with no sacrifice in quality. This will yield you tremendous price savings.

Any stone you see with the trademark **Rock of Ages** will likely cost 25-35% more than an equivalent stone without it. This is not worth the extra expense.

Granite Markers

A good way to select a stone and a company is to get out and look at stones at the various cemeteries. Check the quality of workmanship, contrast of lettering, conditions of the stone itself, effects of pollution, erosion or staining. Is it level or has it sunk into the ground? Once you have an idea of what you want, drive around to the various monument companies. Your funeral home or cemetery in most cases can sell you monuments, but make them be competitive by shopping around and knowing your prices. There is a margin here to work with.

Usually the lighter color of stone the deeper it must be engraved for contrast and the more difficult/expensive it will be to grind off an error and re-engrave. If the purchaser, be it the family member, funeral home or cemetery gives the stone company incorrect information, the stone company is not responsible for the error. If the stone company is at fault they are responsible to correct the error with no cost to you. Epoxy is used sometimes to correct errors, rather than start over again on a new stone. This is not the best choice as epoxy may discolor over time due to weather conditions. Ask to see a sample before accepting this option. It's to your benefit to deal directly with the stone companies, (rather than through a funeral director or cemetery), both to avoid errors, and to say how they are to correct errors should they occur.

Bronze Marker

Bronze is sold by the inch. A common ploy to get extra income from the uninformed customer is to quote a low price per square inch, then charge for marker measurement plus the extra measurement area of the concrete base as well.

As an example, let's say you purchased a 12" x 24" bronze marker and you paid $450 for the marker. Most concrete bases would add 2 to 4 inches on each of the four sides of the marker. So, rather than a 12" x 24" marker, it suddenly becomes a 16" x 28" marker. What you *should* see on your bill of sale is a 12" x 24" bronze marker at so much per square inch equals $450 and a setting fee and a concrete base of $85…not a 16" x 28" bronze marker for so much per square inch equals $675.

Marker Maintenance

Some cemetery packages include a statement relating to perpetual care that says in effect that monuments may need shimming every few years to account for settling, though this will vary with the soil at the installation site. If installation was correctly done, it would not have settled or tilted. This is another way that cemetery associations get extra income in the form of *Perpetual Maintenance,* and this is why the cemeteries don't always use concrete footings, when installing their own stones, as an added measure to insure that they won't tilt or settle. They will wait until you contact them about settling stones and charge you a fee for resetting. Cemetery rules and regulations are kind of like Covenants Conditions & Restrictions in a subdivision. As the customer, you could pay for and demand the concrete footings or find a cemetery that will go along with your specifications.

It is important that you know what you are buying before you agree to anything. Be well informed, and ask questions.

Monument technology has advanced over the years. If you can envision it, someone can make it. New technology has opened up the door to fantastic advances in monuments, with laser-guided etchings, portraits, and photographs. If you have something in mind, ask if it can be done. You might be pleasantly surprised at what is available.

9

What to Expect
at a
Traditional Funeral Service

Personal Effects of the Deceased

What to Bring to the Funeral Home

If you decide to have the deceased embalmed, you should bring clothing with you to the funeral home for the burial.

Whatever the deceased wore during life would be appropriate in death. Items to consider would be a favorite dress or suit, jewelry, wig or hair pieces, false teeth, eye glasses, socks, panty hose and under garments.

If the gentleman never wore a suit, ask yourself, what did he wear and feel comfortable in? Perhaps it was overalls, sport coats, sweaters or maybe slacks and sport shirt. Some men wear French cuffs with links. Some like tie bars, lapel pins and other jewelry for men.

What to Remove After the Service

It is usually customary after the chapel service for the funeral director to remove and return to the family any rings and other jewelry that will not be buried with the deceased.

Written instruction should be given to the funeral director as to what personal effects stay with the deceased and what effects should be removed and given back to the family before burial. If possible, appoint a family member or friend to make sure that everything requested is returned to you.

Eyeglasses are often donated to the Lions Clubs or other non-profit organizations, unless otherwise specified.

What Things Do You Want Buried or Cremated with the Deceased?

Sometimes family members want little things to be with the deceased like notes, drawings or letters from the grandchildren. I have had requests for such things as favorite fishing poles, golf clubs, six-packs of beer — almost anything that the family wants could be accommodated.

Hair and Cosmetics

One of the favorite phrases of the funeral directors is to "create a memory picture". A recent photograph of the deceased is helpful to the staff hairdresser.

> **For Women:** Funeral homes have people available to do women's hair. This would be an extra charge. Another choice is a family member who would be willing and able to do the hair of the deceased. Perhaps you could ask the deceased's own hairstylist to do her hair. However, they must be willing and able. Bring the deceased's special shade of lipstick or any other make-up you desire.

> **For Men:** Communicate to the funeral director in regards to the gentleman's facial hair. Did he wear a beard or mustache? Was he clean shaven? This information is helpful to the funeral director so that they don't shave off hair that should be there or leave hair that should be removed. If the deceased was in a hospital for a period of time before death, he may not have shaved for several days. It is a good idea to suggest a trim around the ears if that is in order.

For the Death Certificate, most states need to know the mother's maiden name of the deceased.

Sometimes, a veil is used to cover the face if the deceased had suffered a long illness or other tragedy. Consider using gloves for the hands that do not bring dignity to the deceased. Most funeral homes have veils available that would cover the entire open end of the casket. Again, to provide some dignity to the deceased.

The Service

The Funeral Ceremony

No attempt will be made to cite the diversity of funeral customs among the world's two thousand-plus religions. Get with your family, the person you are making the arrangements for while there's time, and your minister, priest, rabbi, etc., and decide how the ceremony will be performed.

A good way to plan this is to allot a time period for the whole ceremony and work within it. Perhaps somewhere between thirty to sixty minutes as a span for the entire affair.

> There is no right way to remember a deceased member of the family.
>
> Just keep in mind that, no matter what the service is, **it is for the living.**

If there's to be three hymns sung, at a little over three minutes each, there's ten minutes accounted for. Give the minister ten to fifteen minutes, another five minutes for prayers or communal reading of scriptures, and perhaps five to ten minutes for each eulogy. You can arrange these segments in any order to suit you.

Some religions have a prescribed funeral ceremony, which will go on for a great deal longer. And by their very nature would be more costly as the more activities you have the more expense for using the facilities and its personnel may be incurred.

Some will prefer to have several friends and family members get up and say a few words. Some like more hymns, a soloist or choir, communion, an instrumental number with silent introspection, and a range of other options.

The point is, make the ceremony personal, or better yet, make it what the deceased had requested, assuming you had the time to get their input…no more, no less. There is no right way to remember a deceased member of the family. Just keep in mind that, no matter what the service is, *it is for the living.*

Before the Funeral

Preceding the actual funeral service there are hours, or in some cases days, during which friends and family will stop by to pay their respects, visit with other mourners, and view the deceased at the funeral home. This is assuming you have elected to have the deceased available for viewing.

Viewing can take place on the day or evening before the service, just before the service, and the casket closed during the service and then opened again for viewing before going to the cemetery.

Most funeral homes discourage viewing at the cemetery; because of the natural sunlight would cause the deceased to look unpleasant and this could be upsetting. In the funeral homes they use artificially colored lights to help in making the deceased look as natural as possible.

Since we are living longer these days, it is becoming increasingly common for the deceased to request there NOT be a viewing due to the devastating effects of a long illness. As with the case of a severe trauma related death (for example an automobile accident), the family and/or deceased may wish a portrait or photograph be placed upon the closed casket instead of having a direct viewing.

In fact, several studies show trends are heading toward having a **direct burial or cremation** (the deceased taken from the place of death directly to the cemetery or crematory), with a modest ceremony held later at a church, chapel, graveside, golf club, or in the home.

It is somewhat expected that as many as half of all funerals will involve the usual several days of viewing and visitation. In theory, this is to give distant friends and relatives time to travel to the site. In practice, it drives the economics of funerals sky high and adds to the emotional burden on the grieving family by extending things for several days during which they will have to recount everything concerning the deceased's passing numerous times over. Viewing periods should be attended, as a rule, by at least one member of the deceased's family and should be scheduled for the convenience of those wishing to pay their respects.

Someone in the family should put visitors at ease during these visits. Although there will be plenty of time for open mourning at the funeral, every moment involved does not have to be filled with grieving. Laughter and talking openly about the deceased is good therapy for all.

Sometimes old friends and relatives from long ago will be drop by and will want to extend their conversations beyond the passing of the deceased. Nothing could be more natural. For this reason, whatever the charge for common areas such as a kitchen, coffee lounge, or parlor is well worth the money spent.

The family will value some distraction and a visit from an old friend bringing each other up to date on their lives, telling stories, reminiscing about old times, even exchanging jokes. This time well spent and is part of the healing process.

An alternative that works nicely is to have family extend an invitation for people who come for visitation to drop by the home for refreshments after the viewing. Here there will be ample time for story telling and reminiscing in familiar surroundings.

Graveside Services At the Cemetery

If your choice is cremation, you can skip this part unless you have elected to have the ashes interred in the cemetery. Now that you have decided where the burial is to take place, let's go over what you want to do there as part of the service.

If the actual funeral service is held elsewhere, the cemetery portion may be attended by just the family or open to all. The finality of the deceased actually going into the ground tends to heighten emotions, so some prefer limiting the graveside portion to just family.

Some elect to have a simple prayer while the casket sits on a device over the grave, then depart while it is enclosed and filled-in. They return later to situate floral pieces, take photographs, and so forth.

When the services are open to all, members who wish to stay may participate in the ancient custom of tossing in a handful of soil after the casket is lowered into the grave. Again, it is your choice, but be sure to remember that graveside services are particularly hard on those who must get around with walkers or in wheelchairs, so have plenty of assistance available.

If you elect graveside services, the event will take place at the grave, so you will need chairs and a tent, which may be provided as part of a cemetery package.

In some parts of the country, because of the adverse weather, the services cannot be held at the gravesite and will be moved to another location of the cemetery that will provide shelter for family and friends.

For veterans, the graveside portion of the funeral is particularly emotional. The rifle salute followed by a bugler playing Taps, and concluding with the formal folding and presentation of the flag is moving regardless of what your stand on military service may be. Furthermore, it is an honor earned for a service rendered to our country.

There is often an uneasy moment just after the graveside service. The formal part of the ceremony is largely over, yet often people are reluctant to leave and uncertain what protocol to follow if they stay. One should endeavor to offer final condolence to the family before departing, but not in a constant parade like the receiving line at a banquet. The family can define the course of action at this point by having the minister say something to this effect:

> **"The family would like to express its sincerest appreciation
> for each of you coming today and for your generous acknowledgments
> of their loss. They look forward to thanking each
> of you personally over the coming weeks."**

At the end of the service, the minister can either issue an invitation to a reception being held later, or wish everyone a safe drive home as the family wishes. This lets everyone know the ceremony is complete and frees the friends to go their separate ways. This is much better than having people standing around wondering what to do next.

Traveling To the Cemetery

How will you get to the cemetery? Most funeral homes have limousines available (for a fee) for the immediate family. Additional limousines provided by the funeral home will be available at a slightly inflated rental rate. You can choose to hire them directly from an independent limousine company yourself. A cost savings option here would be renting an upscale automobile from a rental agency or car dealership and having a relative drive. Either way, you'll need to decide who rides with whom in advance so no one is left behind especially those needing support for health reasons or those emotionally overcome.

Police Escort

The funeral director generally arranges for this and there may be a fee. Years ago in major cities the local police would provide escorts. Now it is a business. The charge is anywhere from $50 to $100 per escort rider, usually with a minimum of two riders.

If you live in a rural community, you can inquire about it yourself or just phone the nearest precinct or sheriff's office. Often such services are provided to rural taxpayers at no charge.

Another alternative to save some costs is for family and friends to meet at the cemetery at the appointed time. Make certain everyone knows that the vehicles carrying the *immediate family* and those requiring assistance will have the priority parking spaces nearest the site.

Conclusion of Funeral Services

It is not uncommon for family, friends, and neighbors to walk in single file past the deceased for a final viewing following the funeral service. If this is to be the case, soft music in the background is simple to arrange by just requesting it at the time of the funeral arrangements. Your choices include recorded organ, recorded organ and vocal, live organ, and live organ and vocal. There is usually an extra charge for recorded music and honorarium fees for live organ and vocal.

Since this will likely be the last time the casket is opened, the family may want to remain for a few minutes to say their good-byes before departing the funeral home chapel or church.

Between the time the family exits the chapel and the funeral procession is ready to leave for the gravesite, the funeral director's staff has some things to do. First, they must close the casket, and then there will be floral arrangements to pack into a van for the trip to the cemetery. They may want to depart ahead of the family to ensure everything is in readiness at the cemetery when family and guests arrive. You must coordinate this with the funeral director.

Pallbearers

The family normally selects the Pallbearers who might be best friends, business associates or friends of the family. It would normally be an honor to serve as a pallbearer. Under normal circumstances six (6) people would be used. Grandchildren often serve as pallbearers for their grandparents. If the deceased is quite old, oftentimes friends in the same age bracket are unable to physically serve so the family will list them as honorary pallbearers. Their listing is done if memorial folders are used and the pallbearers are normally listed in the folder as well as the honorary.

In your selection of pallbearers, physical condition should be considered, as the duties of the pallbearers include carrying the casket from the outside of the funeral home chapel or church to the awaiting hearse, which is mostly lifting because the casket is on a funeral dolly. However, at the cemetery this is another matter. Some cemeteries do not provide dollies, and the hills could be steep near the grave, and at times there could be a little walk to the location of the grave from where the hearse has to park.

Last Minute Preparations Before Traveling to The Cemetery

Feel free to join friends and family outside or in the lobby during the time that the funeral director is making final preparations to leave the funeral home chapel to go to the cemetery.

Ask the funeral director to let you know when you need to start for the limousine or your automobile. If pallbearers are used, when they exit from the chapel with the casket is usually the signal.

You need to decide in advance who will ride with whom, who will need assistance, and each car's position behind the hearse and police escort.

If you've decided you would be more comfortable having only the immediate family at the cemetery, by all means have either the minister or the funeral director announce this prior to the beginning of the service, so there'll be no misunderstanding. He can include it in a general "thank you for coming out" statement so no one will be slighted, or even report to those attending about the scarcity of seating or parking (as at some mausoleums) as a regrettable reason for having to limit participation to just the family. If a private family graveside is desired, this information can also be printed on the service folder as well to alleviate any misunderstandings.

Children and Funerals

There is no hard and fast rule on how young is too young to attend a funeral, but there's a wealth of advice out there about how to deal with children and death. Family Communications publishes a series of booklets on the subject (the **Lets Talk About It** series,) as well as videotape programs. The booklet entitled "**Talking with Young Children about Living and Dying**" is well done, as is the video tape narrated by TV's Fred Rogers, (Mr. Rogers) who touches upon many of children's concerns. It may be available at your local library, Hospice center, or even through some of the more progressive funeral homes. You can call Family Communications, Inc. at (412) 687-2990.

Behavior Expectations

As to modes of behavior and etiquette at the viewing area or at the funeral service itself, there really are no guidelines; you can be strong or stricken, but be yourself.

Visiting with Friends & Relatives

At the Funeral Home or Your Home

Having another relative on the scene to relieve the widow or widower so that they can go to the parlor/kitchen to be with these relatives and friends in less emotional surroundings is paramount.

Another suggestion would be to station a relative near the guest register so he/she gets the name of the visitor and introduces them to the next of kin. This is particularly important with the elderly who don't need the added stress of wondering who that person is.

There is another good reason to hold the number of viewing periods to a minimum. They take so much out of the survivors that, by the time the actual funeral ceremony is held, they are often too fatigued to feel much of anything beyond relief. See to it that the closest family members and the more emotional friends, get adequate rest and time away from the viewing area.

There are many caterers who would be more than happy to put on most any sort of spread you will pay for, but it is neither necessary nor expected. For the viewing periods, be it at a funeral home chapel, church annex, or your own home, coffee and perhaps some cookies is plenty. In many areas of the country it is customary for friends, neighbors, and relatives to bring offerings of food, and these are very well received along with the coffee.

If you would prefer a wake or perhaps a reception following the services, by all means go ahead, but keep the fare reasonable.

Who Should You Notify?

Notification List

You need a list of family and friends to notify of death of the loved one. The more complete and current this list the easier this particular task will be. We have provided a template for you to copy in the Forms Section for your convenience. Our suggestion is to have a separate page for each geographic area, which will be easier to divide up among the family members who have accepted notification responsibility. Compile this list as soon as possible and when the time comes, delegate the person at the head of each list to phone everyone below them. You can hand them a copy, fax it, or read it over the telephone, this method will allow extra time for other decisions.

In the case of the anticipated death, the news will be easier to accept on the other end provided that you have advised everyone of the deceased's condition beforehand. For the truly close or ailing, you might want someone to be with them for support when they are notified of the death. This is a particular consideration for those with significant medical histories.

Ex Spouses

How do you list an ex-husband, or ex-wife among the survivors? Some don't! For others, especially those who had children with this person or remained relatively close after divorcing, inclusion of the Ex seems natural enough. Again, ask. How did the deceased want it? Ask the deceased beforehand if possible to put it in writing. If it is not possible to ask the deceased, the immediate family is next in line to make that decision.

Newspaper Notice (Obituary)

How would the deceased like his or her name to appear in print? It bears discussion, as does how one would have the engraving on a headstone read. Address this topic early since it will have a most important effect, both in the immediate future and forever.

There are a lot of other things to consider in the Notice. Will the cause of death be cited? It varies with newspaper and the family's wishes, unless you take the initiative to state one way or the other in advance.

Often something generic as "following an extended illness" will suffice without getting into the particulars. This is especially important in the case of suicide, homicide, some types of accidental death, and death from some diseases.

How will the survivors be listed? "She is survived by her husband, Michael Scott Higgins", or, Survivors include her husband of fifty years, Michael Scott Higgins, and two daughters Betty Jean Brown of Tempe and Theresa Mitchell of West Lynn, along with six grandchildren." Either way is acceptable, but some guidelines would assist whoever must sit down and draft the newspaper notice.

**Questions You Should Ask of Any
Pre-Pay / Pre-Purchase Funeral Plan**

1. What if I move? Are the benefits transferable?

2. What if the funeral home goes out of business before I die, will I receive a refund?
   And if so, will it include interest?

3. What if my accrued benefits are more than the funeral package selected, who will
   receive the excess funds?

4. Do you have a photograph of the model of casket I selected? (Get a specific model
   number, style of interior. Any extras should be specified and attach all this
   information to your contract or receipt.)

10

What to Do
before Death Happens

Making Arrangements for the Terminally Ill.

The terminally ill are often prone to fanciful excursions when contemplating their funerals, and this is particularly true in the cases of heavily medicated patients. These excursions will range from near total disregard to "Just toss me into a ditch somewhere" to intricate planning that includes engraved invitations and a seating chart. Somewhere between these extremes lies reality.

Get input on the relevant details such as what clothing they would prefer, favorite hymns, songs, or poems they'd like read or sung, which clergyman to handle the service, preference of burial or cremation and where.

You might also ask if there is anything in particular they would like to mention in the obituary or on their headstone. Don't dwell upon the topic too long or the answers will likely get increasingly depressing, but most people **really would** like a say in the arrangements of their own funerals. After all, they've made decisions all their lives.

Speak with the attending physician once the person's condition has defined itself, but don't expect to hear a date certain such as "She only has three weeks." Discuss the person's condition with members of the family as far in advance as possible, to let them know the situation and to prepare them for the inevitable.

You can get down to the actual planning in rough form at first and with definition later. Pre-planning will not only save money, it will also free your mind of much of the added stress at a time when you most want to concentrate on the departed and be with friends and family.

Given the time to plan, it would benefit you greatly to start at the end and work your way back. Begin with the question, where will the remains rest once it's all over? If cremation is elected, will the ashes be dispersed somewhere or retained in an urn or other container? If retained, **who** will keep them? Be specific, ill feelings have resulted from misunderstandings. Scattering of the remains offers an out when there is a conflict over who will retain the cremains.

If burial is elected, **the final destination** is a cemetery. If your family, church, or community has its own cemetery, which is fairly common in rural areas, this can be quite simple. If you live in an urban setting, there's some research to be done, if the dying person doesn't already have a plot or crypt. Please review the cemetery section for some useful hints on how to save money and avoid problems.

Here are some things to consider:
➢ If it is the spouse that you are buying for, do you plan to be buried along side?
➢ What if you re-marry?
➢ What if you move?

All of these things should be considered with a clear head. Burial plots are not cheap, and it makes no sense buying a double plot if only one will be used. Check the classified ads for pre-sold plots.

Telephone the cemetery and get the answers to <u>these</u> questions <u>before</u> you visit the cemetery.

- ➢ What is the price range of your burial plots?
- ➢ Get actual figures, not averages.
- ➢ How do prices vary, geographic location within the cemetery, proximity to walkways or statuary, gardens, etc?
- ➢ Do you require a particular type of vault or liner? If so, do you provide it in the price of the plot or is it additional? If additional, how much? My relative has a pre-planned burial program that may provide the vault, is this allowed or must we purchase yours?
- ➢ What is the cost of opening and closing a grave and how does it vary throughout the day and week and holidays?
- ➢ Does the cemetery require a certain type of monument? If so do you provide it or can I purchase my own from another source? What is the price, dimensions, installation fees, etc.?
- ➢ What are your visitation policies?
- ➢ What is the cemetery's policy on decoration of the graves in terms of flowers, flags and so-forth.
- ➢ Does the cemetery provide chairs and a tent cover for services at the grave? And if not what are the charges for those services?

As the funeral industry evolves from being primarily family owned to conglomerates, you will see more and more instances where the funeral home, cemetery, crematory, and monument company are all under one roof. This should bring economies to scale and **could and should** allow lower overall prices, but this is not the case. Instead, it is used to put economic pressure on the consumer.

For instance, if you want a cremation, there's apt to be one price if the services are handled by the crematory owner's funeral home and another price if the services are handled by another funeral home. (In many cases it is often cheaper when handled elsewhere, but there is likely to be additional fees charged at the funeral home, such as a Cremation Charge in addition to the other crematory's Cremation Fee.)

As an example, say you are using ABC funeral home and they are doing the services followed by cremation. Let's also say that this funeral home is located on the grounds of the cemetery that also has a crematory, all under the same management. ABC cremation fee is $200, but in your shopping around you find a crematory across town (Jones) that charges a cremation fee of only $75. You tell ABC funeral home that you want your father cremated at Jones crematory. ABC will then say, if that's your desire, we have a $200 transportation fee to Jones. Here you still have options. Maybe Jones can provide more reasonable transportation or ABC in an effort to keep your business, may be willing to reduce their charges.

A "Wal-Mart type of marketing strategy " could be on the move in the funeral industry. It happens in other industries and could easily happen in the funeral industry as well. Don't be surprised to see conglomerate funeral homes and other funeral-related industries move into a moderate size town and under-sell all the family owned businesses for a couple of years to drive them out of business, or at least certain segments of it. Then the prices will go back up even higher than before.

The conglomerate today is 25 to 30% higher than most local funeral homes, so they could well afford to drop their normal prices lower than the local funeral home for a period of time knowing that they could eliminate or reduce the competition. Then they raise the prices back to their normal 25 to 30%, or higher, than the locals do. This could possibly eliminate any choice for the consumer in the future.

Watch out for promotional items such as "We open and close the grave for "free" or "Our limousine service is provided at no cost to the immediate family." Expect to **really pay** for something else to make up for it.

After you have made your calls and done your comparison shopping, go and interview the company personally. If you find one you particularly like, but find it is more costly than another, don't be afraid to mention this fact in dealing with the sales person. Say something like this, " Forest Lawn is much closer to our home, but Cedar Creek is $500 less for a similar plot and that is closer to my budget. If you can see your way clear to lower the price into my price range, we can probably work something out."

At this point you are buying real estate and the salesman will know this. If you wait until after the death occurs, you'll be buying peace of mind and the answer to an immediate problem, and he'll know that also. **Don't be afraid to make your own offer and don't be afraid to walk away if they won't deal.** The salesperson's commission is likely in the 25-45% range, so there's room for some compromise, and you can bet he'll know that as well.

Know in advance that there are at least two prices for everything you see at a cemetery. There's the *At-Need* price, which is what you'll pay if you wait until the individual is deceased and your need is pressing, and it is the highest of all. Then there's the *Pre-Need* price, which is about what it sounds like; something purchased well in advance of actual use. The pre-need prices may be as low as half the at-need price. Then there's the *Absolute* price, which is what you can get if you take the time to research the other cemeteries and you bargain a bit. This can be the lowest price of all.

11

Pitfalls of Pre-Arranging

Now you are aware of what goes into a funeral arrangement, and you know how to shop for the best price and quality of merchandise and services. The next step is to see if everyone you named as potential pallbearers or minister will be available when your time comes, or if they are physically up to the task. You may wish to address this problem in advance on your own or on a loved one's behalf.

For your support we have put together some checklists. We have also prepared some additional information, and some considerations most professionals in the funeral industry would just as soon you didn't address due to the cost considerations involved.

Once again, take your time! Make your phone calls and visits, and do as much as possible while this information is fresh in your mind. Getting your spouse or relative's input is important and valuable. But remember, it's your decision that counts, and the minor depression you might be feeling during this process will weigh lightly against the sense of accomplishment and peace of mind you'll feel having arrangement decisions set down in writing. Don't forget, write it in pencil. See our suggested "My Pre-Arranged Funeral Instructions" form in the Forms Section to help you with these details.

If you did all this work and planning, and didn't tell anyone, what good is the plan? **Let several people know, especially your attorney and next-of-kin, where you keep these details**, whether in your safe, safety deposit box at your bank, or in the family Bible, or wherever, *just tell people!*

Okay, say you have put this information in a safe. Who has access and the combination? If it's in your bank safety deposit box, at *which bank*, and where are the keys? Also, what if death occurs on Friday after banking hours? Will it be Monday **after all major decisions have been made** before anyone can get at these instructions? It would be a good idea for you to make several copies of these instructions and give them to relatives and friends. Some of the information is rather personal so you might want to limit some access. Whatever you decide to do, make certain someone knows where to find your information in a timely fashion.

Ready to begin? Get your pencil and send this first document to one or more persons of your choice.

(Refer to our suggested "Cover Page to My Pre-Arranged Funeral Instructions" form located in the Forms Section as a guide to help you with these details.)

> **Please tell**
>
> **someone**
>
> **what you have**
>
> **accomplished.**
>
> **Don't Keep It a Secret!**

Pre-Payment Plans:

One of the keys to controlling future funeral and cemetery costs is to arrange and pay for them in advance. **Why?** Because people will purchase more in an emotionally charged situation at time of death than they will in a calmer and more stable pre-need moment.

Cemeteries lead the way in offering pre-need products, but nearly all funeral homes are being lured by the tremendous sums of money available. Pre-payment plans are being aggressively sold in the home, by phone and through the mail. Some $20 billion is already invested in various types of pre-payment plans. The majority of this money is in two types of basic products: **Insurance Policies and Trust Funds.**

Little is being done to monitor these funds or the people in charge of them. At the present time, there are no federal laws regulating pre-payment plans and products. The Federal Trade Commission (FTC) is responsible for enforcing the Funeral Rule, but that limited regulation addresses only funeral expenses and does not cover the sales of most pre-payment plans.

While its purview covers deceptive trade practices, the FTC has not taken it upon itself to actively pursue the matter of pre-payment fraud. One bit of good news if you are under pressure to sign a pre-payment contract is the FTC's "Cooling-Off" Rule that gives buyers three business days to cancel a contract *signed in the consumer's home or otherwise away from the seller's place of business.* **Hence, if you signed the contract at the place of business, no cooling off period is allowed.**

So, who is in charge? In some states, the responsibility for inspection falls with the banking commissions, while in others it's vested in the state funeral/cemetery boards which in most cases are only extensions of the industry as the majority of members are professionals from funeral businesses. In the states where there are neither boards nor agencies specifically assigned to oversee the pre-arranged funds, the task usually falls to the attorney generals of each state.

What Are You Pre-Arranging?

A cemetery pre-arrangement can consist of graves, mausoleum crypts, memorials, and sometimes the opening and closing of the graves or crypts. Once you sign a contract the cemetery gives you a deed for the graves and certificates of ownership for the merchandise purchased. The deed is not a deed for the property itself, rather a deed for the interment rights of that grave (you only have the right to inter dead human remains in the property, nothing else).

Some cemeteries may want to charge you interest over the term of your contract. This is legal but not right. You may not think anything about being charged interest because we have become accustomed to buying cars, homes, washers, and dryers on installment plans. The difference is that you take these items home with you and use them throughout the life of the contract. You may not have need for the cemetery grave, vault and marker for years after making the purchase, so don't let a fast talking salesperson dupe you in to paying interest. Your options would be to go to another cemetery if one is available. Your next choice would be a funeral home who would include the cemetery goods and services on a pre-arrangement contract. Most funeral homes normally do not charge interest.

A funeral pre-arrangement is normally comprised of a casket or some type of container, plus whatever type of services that are selected (e.g., embalming, cremation, visitation, transportation, memorial services etc.) The funeral package may, in some cases, also include a vault and a monument/grave marker or "memorials" as they are sometimes called.

Insurance Policies

Most every funeral home and cemetery is affiliated with some type of insurance company. The insurance companies are highly regulated and are usually more balanced and more stable than most funeral homes and cemeteries. Even when insurance companies go bankrupt, state and federal agencies often come to the rescue of the policyholders. You cannot say the same about funeral homes and cemeteries.

Three types of insurance policies:

Dollar-For-Dollar Coverage

This is where the insured pays, for example, $4,000 in premiums for the policy with a face value of $4,000. Assuming that today's funeral would cost $4,000, about the only positive with this type is that the customer is making some pre-arrangements. The negatives are that the customer has grossly overpaid for the policy and still has no guarantee that the face value of the policy will cover the cost of the funeral when it eventually occurs. You would be well served to stay away from this type of policy because of the lack of risk on the part of the insurance company. All you are doing is exchanging dollars with the insurance company. You have also lost the use of your money (you could have earned interest in a bank account) over this period of time, and there is no inflation clause in this policy.

Today's Dollars for Tomorrow's Funerals

The insured pays about $4,000 in premiums for a policy with the face amount of $6,000. In addition to making pre-arrangements, the only other positive is that the customer's estate will get money back if the cost of the funeral is less than that of the policy's face amount. The negatives still outweigh the positives. The consumer has again overpaid for the policy and there is no guarantee that the policy will cover the eventual costs of the funeral. This is much better than the first example, but not a very good bargain for you. The only way that this is a good deal is if you die within the first few years of the policy.

Insurance That Grows In Value

Here the insured pays about $1,900 in premiums for a policy with a face amount of $4,000 (for this example, the estimated cost of a funeral today). This is the best possible type of coverage. This type of policy is designed to increase in face value at roughly the rate of inflation. If insurance is the way you choose to go, then you have made pre-arrangements and received the most value for the dollars invested here. If the insurance is financially sound and the funeral director guarantees that the policy will cover the cost of the funeral no matter when it occurs, there really are no negatives to this type of coverage.

Questions You Should Ask About Insurance Policies:

➢ What are the premiums vs. the face value of the policy?

➢ Is the policy guaranteed to cover the cost of the service and merchandise you've selected? (Do not accept the policy if it is not *guaranteed* by the funeral home to cover the cost.)

➢ What is the growth potential of the policy?

➢ What is the rating of the insurance company?

➢ What state agency oversees insurance sales in your state? (Contact that agency and request information on the company.)

➢ What commission is being paid? (The salesperson has to answer!)

➢ Who is the beneficiary? (It should be the funeral home, and not your estate if you want to avoid taxation. However the funeral home MUST GUARANTEE that the policy will cover the services and merchandise selected.)

Most cemeteries and well over half of all the funeral homes are now selling some type of pre-need plan. Some of the leaders in the pre-need insurance industry are as follows.

American Funeral Assurance   Pan Western Life

Brookings International Life Insurance Company   Pierce National Life

Forethought Life   United Family Life

Homesteaders Life

Trust Funds

Between 30% and 70% of the money you invest in a cemetery pre-arrangement contract (varies by state) is required to be set aside in a trust fund to cover the price of the merchandise purchased. Funeral plans are often required to trust much higher amounts, as high as 100%. The difference between the two is business philosophies. Funeral homes prefer the higher amount as it tends to lock in the customer and it inhibits competition, as it's hard to sell against an investment in which nearly all of the customer's money is placed in trust.

All 100% of my funds trusted is a strong argument on behalf of the customer. Even with all the money placed in trust, this act does not guarantee the customer that the funds invested will actually cover the cost of the funeral.

Revocable vs. Irrevocable Trusts

Consumers, even those dependent upon Social Security and who qualify for Medicare and Medicaid, can establish an *irrevocable* (i.e., the money cannot be removed) *trust,* bank account, or insurance policy provided the funds are used exclusively for funeral and cemetery expenses. An alternative for those folks is to set up a *revocable trust* (i.e., the money can be removed). It must be one or the other.

Totten Trust

People can place money in trust for themselves and avoid the funeral director and the cemetery sales people altogether. Here you are in control of how and where the money is invested. The disadvantage to this approach is that it leaves the money in the estate exposed to taxation, and if there are too many assets in the estate, there is potential problems qualifying for Medicare and Medicaid benefits.

Another approach is to find a funeral home or cemetery that has an established trust account at a local financial institution that provides trusteeship of the monies. As trustee, the financial institution will be entitled to collect some fees, but that would be a reasonable trade-off for receiving good management of the monies. Be leery of pre-arrangement contracts in which an independent individual or individuals, like funeral homes or cemetery operators, oversee the monies in the trust fund.

Some states have master trusts associations in which many funeral homes participate. They are usually managed in a very conservative manner and have not realized the returns of the more progressive trusts. This may be a very good option though, as long as the funds keep up with inflation.

The negative side of this approach, if the amount in the individual trust fund is insufficient to pay for the services and merchandise that was ordered, the family will be forced to pay the balance. A couple of other things to consider with the master trusts, is paying someone to manage the monies, and that often the association receives some type of kick-back fee somewhere in the neighborhood of .25% to .5% of the monies invested.

Questions You Should Ask About Pre-Need Trusts

➤ Who is the trustee of the fund? (It is a conflict of interest for someone in the funeral home or cemetery to be the trustee, although this is allowed in some states, due to strong industry lobbying.)

➤ Who sets up the trustee fee? (Is it the funeral home, cemetery, or an outside person)?

➤ How much are the trustee fees? (.7% to 1.25% maximum, the higher amount trusted, the lower the fee should be; larger trustee fees often indicate that there are kickbacks being paid to the funeral homes, cemetery, association, or someone.)

➤ What investments have been made by the trusts? Ask for a listing of the investments. If the trust is invested in mutual funds, be aware these funds might charge their own fee 2% to 5% plus another 1% to 2% annually. If the trust is invested in high-fee mutual funds, better look for another option.

➤ What are the historic returns on the trusts monies invested?

➤ Is the trust portable? (It should be a plan recognized and accepted throughout the United States whereby the monies can be used item-for-item, and *without penalty*, by any other funeral and cemetery facility that you choose.

➤ What state agency, if any, oversees the trust fund? (Then ask the agency for a report on the trust fund. With this report you will learn a lot about the fund, and will show you when the fund was last audited.)

➢ Can family members change the funeral arrangements you make? And, if so, *what can you do* to prevent that from happening?

➢ Is this an individual trust fund? (It shouldn't be unless required by law. The fees will probably be higher and you would want to avoid this type.)

➢ Is it a revocable or irrevocable trust? (Can you get your money back?)

➢ Is it federally insured? (Take advantage of this whenever possible.)

Seminars Available

Learn first hand from national speaker, Ralph Hicks, author of

Everyone Dies!
Secrets That Can Save You Thousands in Unnecessary Funeral Costs.

Ralph is available to speak to your Convention, Church and Senior
Citizens Groups, and continuing education for Social Service
and Hospice Professionals.

For Information
Contact Equitable Associates at
1-888-556-1350

Our mission is to empower people with knowledge of their legal rights,
fair pricing, and alternative money-saving options that are not
always offered by the funeral home.

12

Benefits: Social Security
& Veterans

Social Security

A Special, One-Time, Death Benefit in the amount of $255 is payable to the survivor of the deceased who has worked the minimum quarters required by Social Security. To begin the filing process call Social Security at 1-800-772-1213 or your local Social Security Office. Social Security requires a Certified Copy of the Death Certificate. Most counties provide this Certified copy of the Death Certificate at no charge, usually marked (For Government Use Only), your funeral director will request this Certified Copy with additional copies needed for life insurance, bank accounts, etc.

Social Security also provides, at no charge, a booklet entitled Social Security Survivors Benefits that gives an overview of additional benefits for widow or widower benefits, minor children, disability benefits, etc. Call Social Security at 1-800-772-1213 or your local Social Security Office, or they can be reached on the internet @ www.ssa.gov.

Veterans

Some veterans and their immediate family can be buried in national cemeteries, including Arlington National Cemetery. These burial plots are free, but transportation of the remains is left to the family unless the deceased died in active duty. Most national cemeteries also have columbaria or niches, should cremation be elected.

Burial At Sea

If the deceased is an honorably discharged veteran and you would like the ashes dispersed at sea, you can contact the nearest U.S. Navy Medical Center and ask to speak to the *Decedent Affairs Office.*

There is usually no charge for this service by the Navy. The Navy is the only branch of the military that will scatter the ashes at sea at no charge to the family. Usually you must wait until an available ship is made ready and at that time they may scatter several sets of cremains as they are going out on maneuvers. You, however, are responsible for getting the cremains to the ship.

This can be done via UPS, Federal Express, or any other traceable means. No witnesses are allowed on U.S. Ships. I recommend getting a traceable means of forwarding the package.

For burial at sea, contact the departments below:

Retired Activities Section (Pers-662c)
Bureau of Naval Personnel
Washington, D.C. 20370-6620
1-800-255-8950 or 1-703-614-3197

Office of Medical/Dental Affairs
(MEDDEN AFFAIRS (For Retirees)
Mortuary Affairs, Bldg. 3811
Great Lakes, IL 60088-5200
1-800-376-1131 ext. 629

Commandant (G-PMP-2)
U.S. Coast Guard
2100 Second Street, SW
Washington, D.C. 20593-0001
1-800-772-8724 or 1-202-267-2257/2259

Burial in National Cemeteries

For questions and information about burials in National cemeteries, contact the department below.

Superintendent
Arlington, VA 22211-5003
1-703-695-3250/3255

Information Required For Burial In a National Cemetery

➢ Full name and military grade

➢ Uniformed Service (Branch)

➢ Social Security Number

➢ Service number (if applicable and known)

➢ VA claim number (if assigned and known)

➢ Date and place of birth

➢ Date of retirement or honorable separation from active duty

➢ Date and place of death

➢ Copy of separation papers (DD Form 214)

VA Burial Allowance and Transportation

Generally, the VA benefits are in the form of reimbursements for the monies you have paid out for the various funeral home or cemetery goods and services. You must contact your nearest Veteran's Administration office to apply for these benefits or call 1-800-827-1000.

The Veteran's Administration has the following cash allowances available:

➢ **Death During Active Duty:**

All funeral expenses will be paid by the military, including body preparation, casket, transportation to the place of disposition, interment (if in a national cemetery), and marker. In addition, the next-of-kin are entitled to a death gratuity up to $6,000.

➤ **Death Due To A Service Related Injury:**

There is a $1,500 burial allowance for these veterans which may be used to cover some of the funeral director expenses, the casket and transportation to the cemetery. If death occurred in a VA facility, transportation of the body to the cemetery will be paid provided it is no further than the last place of residence.

If burial is not in a National Cemetery, there is $150 interment allowance, but it is unlikely that it will cover the cost of the opening/closing of the grave or concrete liner charges, let alone the cost of the lot. A marker is available at no charge, however the private cemetery will probably have a setting fee.

➤ **Non-Service Related Death In A VA Facility or While Collecting a VA Pension or Disability Compensation:**

There is a $300 burial allowance, which may be used to defray some of the usual funeral expenses. Although burial in a National Cemetery is free to these veterans, all funeral home expenses are the responsibly of the family. Transportation to a National Cemetery (not farther than the residence of the deceased), will be provided only if death occurred in a VA facility. An $150 interment allowance applies when burial is in OTHER than a National Cemetery.

➤ **Death of A Veteran OUTSIDE a VA Facility, Not Receiving Military Pension or Compensation:**

The $1,500, $300, $150 benefits DO NOT APPLY, nor is there reimbursement for transportation to the cemetery. A lot in a National Cemetery, opening/closing of the grave, any required concrete liner, a marker, and the United States flag are the only burial benefits available to any honorably discharged veteran, other than as listed above.

If the interment is in other than a National Cemetery, the family is responsible for the cost of the lot, opening/closing of the grave, liner and any fee for setting the marker.

The Veterans Administration requires a Certified copy of the Death Certificate. Most counties provide the Certified copies of the Death Certificate at no charge. These are usually stamped "For Government Use Only". Your funeral director will request a Certified copy and additional copies for life insurance, bank accounts, etc.

Veterans should be aware that a burial site in one of the 114 cemeteries, located in 38 states, **cannot be reserved prior to the time of death.** Application can be filed only at the time of death.

Interment in a National Cemetery is available to all members of the United States armed forces and veterans (honorably discharged); spouses; widows; widowers who did not remarry; minor children; and under certain conditions, unmarried adult children. Also eligible are members of the armed forces reserves who die while on active duty, training for, or performing in the duties of the reserves, or who have 20 years of services in the reserves. The National Cemetery System pays for the opening and closing of the grave at all national cemeteries.

Headstones and Markers

The National Cemetery System also provides headstones and markers. The marker can be flat (made of bronze, granite, or marble) or upright (made of granite or marble). The markers are inscribed with the name of the deceased, dates of birth and death, and the branch of military service. The veteran's marker is provided *free of charge*.

If the person is buried in a cemetery other than a national, military post or state veterans' cemetery, the headstone or marker must be applied for through the United States Department of Veterans Affairs. In such cases, the headstone or marker will be shipped at government expense but the family must pay the cost of installation

You must make application to the following government office and ask for Form 40-1330 (some funeral directors/cemeteries can provide this form).

VA Headstones and Markers
Office of Memorial Programs (403)
Department of Veteran Affairs
810 Vermont Avenue NM
Washington, D.C. 20420
1-800-827-1000

In the past 20 years, the annual interments in National Cemeteries have nearly doubled to over 70,000 per year, and the rate of increase is projected to continue into the early part of the next century as people get older. Many of these cemeteries are at, or near, capacity and all existing national cemeteries are expected to be full by the year 2020. The cemeteries that are full can still accept cremation burials, or inurnment of cremains in columbaria.

Application for Presidential Memorial Certificates

Presidential Memorial Certificates (PMC) can be applied for at your nearest VA Regional office

Military Honors

Almost anyone who served on active duty in the military can receive graveside honors including a rifle salute, the playing of Taps, and the flag ceremony. Phone the nearest military base (including ROTC and Recruiting Stations or veterans organizations). The American Legion, Veterans of Foreign Wars (VFW), and American Veterans (AMVETS) can either provide or direct you to those services.

United States Flag

You can apply to the following government agency to acquire the United States Flag for Veteran's caskets and presentation to the family.

<u>Veterans Administration Flag</u>
Available from nearest VA with completed VA Form 2008
Also available from many post offices, with VA Form 2008
Or call 1-800-827-1000

Comfort with
The Healing Spirit of Watercolor!

Visionary artist, Maajica, creates unique art forms using the medium of watercolor. As she paints, she paints with the spectrum of light. Colors are healing light frequencies, and when they merge together or overlap in her art, they create extraordinary frequencies and symbols for the healing of the body, mind and spirit.

_____ *My personal Spirit Art*

_____ *Spirit Art in Memory of a Loved One*

Receive an original 7-1/2" x 11" watercolor painting ready to mat and frame.
Visit her website: www.spiritart.net

This art is very personal and has special meaning for the recipient.

Order Form

Telephone Orders: (505) 258-4278   E-mail Orders: maajica@usa.net

Postal Orders: Maajica Productions
P.O. Box 1741
Ruidoso, NM 88355-1741

Credit Card Orders: Website: http://www.spiritart.net

Each Spirit Art: $24.95 plus $5.00 shipping & handling
New Mexico residents please add 6.9375% sales tax (or $1.73).

Please send my "Spirit Art" to me at the following address:

Name: _____

Company Name: _____

Address: _____

City: _____ State: _____ Zip: _____

Telephone: (___) _____

13

Forms

We have provided these forms for your convenience to help you in gathering the vital information needed to support your preferences.

Cover Page to "My Pre-Arranged Funeral Instructions"

This is an Instruction Sheet to be sent to family, friends and attorney informing them that you have made, in writing, advance arrangements for your funeral. It also states where this document or copies of this document can be found.

My Pre-Arranged Funeral Instructions

This document template is provided for your convenience to assist you with the pre-planning details of how you want your funeral or memorial service. This form should be filled out and the original placed with your important documents such as your will, life insurance policies, etc. and copies made and sent to your attorney, your spouse, your children or whoever will ultimately make the final arrangements on your behalf.

Notification List

This suggested form is a template for you to copy and fill out to notify friends and relatives of the death of your loved one.

COVER PAGE
to
"My Pre-Arranged Funeral Instructions"

Name: _____

The original copy of My Pre-Arranged Funeral Instructions can be found in the following location:

_____

_____

The following people hold a copy of My Pre-Arranged Funeral Instructions:

Name   _____ Phone: _____

_____ Phone: _____

_____ Phone: _____

                                                       (Witness)

Date: _____   Date: _____

_____   _____
        Signature   Signature

_____   _____
       Print Name   Print Name

My Pre-Arranged Funeral Instructions

My Legal Name: _____

Name: _____
As you want it to appear in the newspaper notice

Address: _____

_____

Date of Birth: _____ Place of Birth: _____

Previous Address: _____

Social Security No.: _____

Military Service: _____ Dates: _____

Awards & Decorations: _____

Last Rank Achieved: _____

Veterans Affairs Claim Number is: _C-_____

Current Occupation: _____

Company: _____ Number of Years: _____

Education, Etc.

College/University: _____ Number of Years: _____

Degree: _____ Year Earned: _____

Clubs/Fraternal Organizations: _____

Social/Civic Organizations: _____

Church Affiliation: _____

Hobbies: _____

My Pre-Arranged
Funeral Instructions, Cont.

Additional Information

Marital Status: _____

Spouses Name: _____

Spouses Maiden Name, if applicable: _____

Father's Name: _____

Mother's Maiden Name: _____

Children: _____ City & State: _____

Children: _____ City & State: _____

Children: _____ City & State: _____

Children: _____ City & State: _____

Children: _____ City & State: _____

Children: _____ City & State: _____

Children: _____ City & State: _____

Grandchildren: _____ _____

Grandchildren: _____ _____

Grandchildren: _____ _____

Grandchildren: _____ _____

Grandchildren: _____ _____

Great Grandchildren: _____ _____

Great Grandchildren: _____ _____

Great Grandchildren: _____ _____

My Pre-Arranged
Funeral Instructions, Cont.

In preparation for my death, and after considerable thought and research I _____

Name

_____

have decided on the following:

Cemetery Choice

Cemetery Preference: _____

I HAVE or HAVE NOT purchased a cemetery grave or crypt space. If so, the paperwork

is attached to this document or included with my personal papers

Located: _____

Disposition of My Body

Disposition of my remains: Ground Burial
                                    Entombment (mausoleum)
                                    Cremation
                                    Donation to Science
                                    Organization _____

If the disposition is cremation, my ashes are to be:

                                    Retained in an urn
                                    Dispersed _____
                                    Dispersed at sea.

Funeral Home Choice

My Funeral Home Preference is: _____

Casket Choice

The casket of my choice is: _____ Mfg.: _____

Color: _____   Model No.: _____

My Pre-Arranged
Funeral Instructions, Cont.

My preference is: ____Metal ____Wood Other: _____

Monument Choice

The name on my monument should read (if applicable):

Name: _____

Color and Size of The Stone: _____

Inscription: _____

_____

_____

Funeral Service Choices

I desire my funeral or memorial service to be:

        Private (family only)
        Graveside service
        Public chapel or church
        Other
        None
        Public viewing
        Closed casket (no viewing)

Location of my funeral or memorial service: _____

_____

I choose the following hymns and other scriptures for my service: _____

_____

I would like the eulogy delivered by: _____

My Pre-Arranged
Funeral Instructions, Cont.

I would like the following pallbearers selected from the following list (as their physical health and availability will allow:

_____   _____

_____   _____

_____   _____

My Religious Preferences

My religious denomination is: _____

My church of preference is: _____

I would prefer the following clergy, if available, to be in charge of my service. Listed in order of preference:

1. _____   2. _____

3. _____   4. _____

Other Items

Color of flowers for my casket spray: _____

My favorite picture of me to use for my memorial service: _____

Special dress, suit, jewelry or other attire: _____

Donations, in lieu of flowers, to my favorite charity, church, organizations, scholarship fund:

_____

_____

_____

_____

My Pre-Arranged
Funeral Instructions, Cont.

Important Information

My Attorney

My attorney is: _____

Address: _____

City, State & Zip: _____

Telephone: _____

Has a copy of my Last Will and Testament: Yes _____   No _____

My Accountant

My accountant/CPA is: _____

Address: _____

City, State & Zip: _____

Telephone: _____

Financial Institutions

I have accounts at the following institutions:

Name: _____

Address: _____ City, State & Zip: _____

Contact Name: _____ Phone No.: _____

Type of Account: _____ Account No.: _____

My Pre-Arranged
Funeral Instructions, Cont.

Name: _____

Address: _____ City, State & Zip: _____

Contact Name: _____ Phone No.: _____

Type of Account: _____ Account No.: _____

Name: _____

Address: _____ City, State & Zip: _____

Contact Name: _____ Phone No.: _____

Type of Account: _____ Account No.: _____

Name: _____

Address: _____ City, State & Zip: _____

Contact Name: _____ Phone No.: _____

Type of Account: _____ Account No.: _____

My Safe Deposit Box

I have a safe deposit box at the following institution(s): _____

The keys are located: _____

Location of Important Documents

My Will: _____

Birth Certificate: _____

Marriage License: _____

Military Discharge (Form DD214): _____

Automobile Registration Certificates: _____

Real Estate Deeds & Titles: _____

My Pre-Arranged
Funeral Instructions, Cont.

Divorce Decree (if applicable): _____

Mortgages & Notes: _____

Stocks & Bonds: _____

Name of Brokerage House: _____

Telephone No.: _____ Contact Person: _____

Income Tax Records: _____

Insurance Policies:

Life Insurance:

Company: _____ Policy No.: _____

Telephone: _____ Agent's Name: _____

Company: _____ Policy No.: _____

Telephone: _____ Agent's Name: _____

Company: _____ Policy No.: _____

Telephone: _____ Agent's Name: _____

Company: _____ Policy No.: _____

Telephone: _____ Agent's Name: _____

Automobile Insurance:

Company: _____ Policy No.: _____

Telephone: _____ Agent's Name: _____

My Pre-Arranged
Funeral Instructions, Cont.

Company: _____   Policy No.: _____

Telephone: _____   Agent's Name: _____

Homeowner's Insurance:

Company: _____   Policy No.: _____

Telephone: _____   Agent's Name: _____

Other Insurance: _____

Other Preferred Dispositions:

Jewelry: _____

Family Heirlooms: _____

Personal Clothing: _____

Pets: _____

House plants: _____

Other Personal Bequests not covered by my Will:

_____

_____

_____

_____

_____

_____

Notification List

Name: _____   Business Phone: _____

_____

Address:_____   Home Phone: _____

City: _____ Zip:_____   Fax: _____

Other Information: _____   E-Mail: _____

Name: _____   Business Phone: _____

_____

Address:_____   Home Phone: _____

City: _____ Zip:_____   Fax: _____

Other Information: _____   E-Mail: _____

Name: _____   Business Phone: _____

_____

Address:_____   Home Phone: _____

City: _____ Zip:_____   Fax: _____

Other Information: _____   E-Mail: _____

Name: _____   Business Phone: _____

_____

Address:_____   Home Phone: _____

City: _____ Zip:_____   Fax: _____

Other Information: _____   E-Mail: _____

Name: _____   Business Phone: _____

_____

Address:_____   Home Phone: _____

City: _____ Zip:_____   Fax: _____

Other Information: _____   E-Mail: _____

Name: _____   Business Phone: _____

_____

Address:_____   Home Phone: _____

City: _____ Zip:_____   Fax: _____

Other Information: _____   E-Mail: _____

Name: _____   Business Phone: _____

_____

Address:_____   Home Phone: _____

City: _____ Zip:_____   Fax: _____

Other Information: _____   E-Mail: _____

14

Glossary of Terms

Air Shipping Container/Tray	An outer cover for the casket required by most airlines when shipping by air. Usually comes in two pieces, a wooden bottom and a cardboard top with straps.
Algor Mortis	After the heart stops beating, the body temperature begins to drop. The temperature will continue to drop until the body reaches the same temperature as the air around it, usually in fewer than three hours.
Alternative Container	A substitute for a casket, usually made from cardboard, or pressed wood, suitable for cremation.
Autopsy	Or postmortem examination, an examination of a body after death for determining the cause of death or the character and extent of changes produced by disease. Often if the deceased has not been under the care of a physician the county medical examiner will require that an autopsy be performed. Also in cases where criminal negligence is involved, the medical examiner will require that an autopsy be performed.
Basic Services Of Funeral Director And Staff	Use of the funeral home, its furnishings, and its employees. This is where much of the overhead of the funeral home is charged to you: visitation room, chapel, flower stands, lighting, kneeling benches, religious icons, the embalming/dressing/hair dressing of the deceased, staff to assist on visitations, staff and drivers to assist during the funeral and burial etc. Save on these charges by having your service elsewhere (local church or synagogue), and pay only the costs of preparing and transporting the body. **The basic service fee cannot include any charges for items that**

the consumer may decline and must be, by law, listed separately on the General Price List.

Burial Clothing

Funeral directors will sell you clothing in which to bury the deceased. Professionally manufactured burial clothing is of lower quality, because it doesn't have to survive many washings and dry cleanings. Most people are buried in their own clothing.

Burial Insurance

Type of insurance sold primarily by funeral homes and cemeteries.

Burial Permit

Issued by the county of death after the signed death certificate has been filed with that county. The cost is minimal.

Cash Advance

Cash advance items, accommodation items, cash disbursement items, all mean the same thing. In order to facilitate the planning and execution of the funeral service, the funeral director will need to make out-of-pocket expenditures for newspaper notices, flowers, clergy honoraria, etc.

Funeral regulations prohibit the funeral director from profiting from these expenses without disclosing the fact to you, the consumer. You alone are the only one that can authorize these expenditures on your behalf. If the actual price is not known at the time of the funeral arrangement, the funeral director must give an estimate of that cost, and as soon as the price is known, give the customer a written statement of the actual charge.

Casket/Coffin

A box in which to bury human remains. It is that and nothing more. Constructed of wood, steel, copper, bronze, fiberglass, cardboard, fiberboard, and a variety of specialty caskets.

Casket Price List

Casket Price Lists contains the prices of the caskets. The CPL must include the retail price of each casket and alternative container stocked by the funeral home. The funeral director must show the CPL to anyone whom, in person, requests information about caskets and their prices.

Cemetery

A place to bury the remains of the dead. There are many types of cemeteries, private cemeteries, public cemeteries, church cemeteries, commercial cemeteries, and national cemeteries.

Cemetery Lot

A piece of land within the confines of the cemetery that the cemetery sells by issuing a deed that gives the right to bury human remains.

Any time you buy a lot in a cemetery you are agreeing to abide by the cemetery's rules and regulations. Though they are important, the consumer seldom reads them. Typically, they are in fine print and laced with legalese. As they are a part of the contract, take time to read them before signing the contract.

Columbaria	Means a vault, a room, or sometimes just a wall with niches in which to place urns containing human cremains.
Cremation Garden	Areas of cemeteries set aside for the below ground burial of urns. The cemeteries usually require the cremains to be inurned in an urn vault below the ground.
Cremation	A kind of disposition of the human remains. The body is placed in cremation ovens called a "retort" which is heated to 1,000 to 1,500 degrees Fahrenheit. The human body is 70 to 80 percent water, and the balance of bones composed primarily of calcium phosphate. The application of the intense heat of cremation first evaporates the water from the body. The flames then incinerate the muscles, organs and flesh. Most of the bone structure will crumble. The actual incineration process takes an average of one to two hours, depending on the temperature inside and the size of the body. The average person when cremated yields six to 10 pounds of cremains.
Crematory	A building that contains a retort or furnace, either powered by electricity or gas. Usually found on the grounds of cemeteries.
Death Certificate	Contains the deceased person's vital information as well as the cause of death. Signed by the physician or medical examiner. It would usually have the type of disposition, burial, cremation and removal from state. **Certified copies of the death certificates** are usually needed for any transfer of real property, bank accounts, insurance policies, stocks or bonds, social security, veterans benefits. Much better to get sufficient quantities at the time of filing rather than having to make application at a later date.
Decomposition	Death is not a pretty picture, but is among the most natural of life's events. The five stages of decomposition are fairly standard, and the length of time of each will vary with the location of the body, and the surrounding temperature and climate. They are the initial stage, putrefaction stage, black putrefaction stage, butyric stage, and finally dry decay, also known as the skeletal stage.

Donation of Body | A body donated to a medical school will be cremated when the school is finished with it and, if desired, the cremains will be returned to the family. By donating your body you will have aided in the education of future medical personnel, and your family will have received the cremation, all at little or no cost.

Embalming | Modern embalming replaces the blood and other fluids of the body with solutions designed to retard decomposition. One or more methods are utilized, arterial embalming or cavity embalming.

Entombment | To place a casketed body in a crypt.

Estate Filing Fee | A finance fee charged by the funeral home or cemeteries who have to wait until the close of probate to be paid.

Flowers | Casket piece is a flower arrangement designed to fit on the foot end of the casket when casket is open. Be sure that the florist uses a water pack base so that the flowers will last longer.

Floral sprays used for funerals also need a water pack. These Usually hang on racks behind the casket or to the side of the casket.

Bowl arrangements of flowers as well as potted plants are used. Sometimes families request boutonnieres for the pallbearers.

Forwarding Remains to Another Funeral Home | This is the fee that the funeral home would charge to ship the body to another state. These charges should be clearly stated on the funeral home's General Price List.

FTC | Federal Trade Commission is the federal governing body that the consumer can complain to if they feel that a funeral home has mislead them.

Federal Trade Commission
Consumer Response Center
Washington, D.C. 20580
202-326-2222
www.ftc.gov

Funeral Packages | This is a way for funeral homes to avoid itemizing prices. While the FTC permits the use of package prices, they must be in addition to and not in place of the itemized prices on the General Price List.

Funeral Rule	The Federal Trade Commission (FTC) developed a trade regulation rule concerning funeral industry practices, which went into effect April 30, 1984. It is called the Funeral Rule; its purpose is to enable consumers to obtain information about funeral arrangements.
Funeral Service	Usually a traditional ceremony with the body present. The service is held in a funeral home chapel, church or synagogue.
General Price List	General Price List (GPL) is a document that must clearly identify and itemize prices for all goods and services, (embalming, service fees, cash advance items, cremation caskets, and required purchases) that a funeral director provides. Funeral directors are required by law to give a copy of their GPL to anyone who inquires in person about their goods, services or prices.
Grave Liner	Sometimes referred to as a rough box. It is a four-sided reinforced concrete box with no bottom and a loose-fitting lid. The grave liner is lowered into the ground before the graveside service and would surround the casket to prevent the ground from sagging.
Grave	Also known as cemetery plot, they can range in price from $95 to $1,200 depending on the location within the cemetery. Most graves are four to five feet deep and three and one half feet wide and eight feet long. You will pay more for hilltop locations, as well as locations near large trees or near walkways. The least expensive will be at the far perimeters of the cemetery.
Graveside Service	A brief committal service that follows a funeral held elsewhere.
Grief Counselor	New name for funeral directors and cemeterians.
Hearse	A vehicle used to transport the casketed body to a church or cemetery.
Honorarium	Payment for services; usually to ministers, priests, organists, soloists.
Immediate Burial	Immediate burial requires no embalming and no viewing. The General Price List (GPL) must include one price for immediate burials in which the casket is provided by the consumer and a separate price when the funeral home provides the casket or alternative container. Information detailing the services and the containers must also be included.

Immediate Cremation	Requires no embalming and no viewing. The funeral home's GPL must quote a price range and must be accompanied by disclosure language about the availability of alternative containers. The GPL also provides one price in instances where the consumer provides the casket or alternative container, and a separate price when the funeral home provides the casket or alternative container.
	If the cremation is done by an outside crematory, the customer should be advised there would be an additional charge for cremation fee added by the outside crematory to the consumer's bill. Or, this could be listed as a Cash Advance item on the funeral home bill.
Immurement	Placing the casketed body in a mausoleum.
Interment	To place the casketed body in the ground.
Inurnment	To place the cremated remains in the ground.
Irrevocable Trust	Can be set up so that the funds will be used exclusively for funeral goods and services and cemetery expenses. Consumers dependent upon Social Security who qualify for Medicare and Medicaid can establish an irrevocable trust, bank account, insurance policy exclusively for this purpose.
Limousine	Used for the immediate family members. In today's funeral market it is usually an extra charge to the family. Many families are making arrangements to use their own cars or those of friends. Some families are renting vehicles of larger size from local rental car companies as a means of saving money.
Loewen Group	One of the big three funeral conglomerates, headquartered in Burnaby, B.C., Canada. In 1995 they owned 791 funeral homes, 180 cemeteries *November 28, 1995, "Sharing the Vision"*.
Mausoleums	Above ground tombs. A cement structure either covered or uncovered and sometimes 10 tiers high that contain crypts to hold the casketed remains of the deceased. Price is predicated on location. Higher prices are charged for eye level as opposed to those on the top and bottom. Also available are community mausoleums that hold large number of caskets in walls surrounding a chapel-like room often with stained glass windows. Crypts are offered end to end, in which two caskets are inserted one after the other and side by sides are wider crypts.

Memorial Gardens	A section of a cemetery. Some are called Memorial Parks. They are distinguished by the fact that all the grave markers are uniform in size and flat and set flush with the ground. The perception upon entering a memorial garden is one of a large, meticulously landscaped and manicured park.
Memorial Service	Usually a ceremony without the body present. Some families use a picture or pictures of the deceased or flowers as a focal point.
Monuments	Are above-ground grave markers, sometimes called memorials, and come in all shapes and sizes. They are made from granite, marble, or bronze. A common grave marker is installed flush with the ground and made of granite, marble and bronze as well.
Motor Escort Officer	In the past the local police department would provide motor escorts from the funeral chapel or church to the cemetery. Today, however, private companies provide this service.
National Cemeteries	Currently comprised of 114 cemeteries located in 39 states and in Puerto Rico; operated by the National Cemetery System. Also, Arlington National Cemetery managed by the United States Army and 24 overseas military cemeteries run by the American Battle Monuments Commission.
Obituaries	There are two types of notices; "free obituaries" and "paid death notices". These appear in newspapers. Most metropolitan newspapers will, at no cost, print the obituaries of the noteworthy as so deemed by the newspaper. Paid death notices are furnished to the newspaper by the funeral home. The longer the notice the higher the cost. The funeral home should pass this charge on to the family as a cash advance item with no mark up.
Opening and Closing the Grave	To dig the grave and close it after the graveside service is concluded. A backhoe operator can open a grave in less than 30 minutes and close it in even less time.
Outer Container List	The Outer Container List contains the prices of the outer burial containers such as vaults or liners. It must include a complete description and the retail prices of each outer burial container offered by the funeral home. The Outer Container List must be shown to anyone requesting information about these items. As with the Casket Price List, the funeral home is not required to give consumers a copy to keep.

Perpetual Care	You pay for this with the purchase price of the cemetery lot. This cost is to cover the landscape maintenance, mowing, weeding, trimming and removal of flowers and leaves, perpetually. **THIS DOES NOT COVER THE GRAVE MARKER.**
Other Preparation of the Body	This fee includes such things as cosmetic and restoration work. Also, if washing and disinfecting are used in lieu of embalming, these charges should be itemized on your invoice from the funeral home.
Pallbearer	It is a solemn obligation and an honor to be asked to bear the casket of a family member or departed friend. Usually six pallbearers serve to bear the casket. The family, in some instances, will want additional bearers and will have honorary pallbearers if these friends are physically unable to serve and will be mentioned has honorary.
Preservative and Protective Value Claims	It is illegal to represent to the consumer that funeral goods or services will delay the natural decomposition of human remains for either a long time or for an indefinite period. It is also illegal to tell consumers that such funeral goods as caskets and vaults possess protective features or will protect the body from gravesite substances. The funeral director is required by federal law to provide the consumer with all manufacturers' warranty information for goods that are purchased. **THE FTC PROHIBITS ANY AND ALL OTHER MISREPRESENTA- TIONS OR DECEPTIVE PRACTICES NOT SPECIFIC- ALLY PROHIBITED BY THE FUNERAL RULE.**
Pre-arranging	To arrange and sometimes pre-pay for funeral goods and services in advance. Cemeteries lead the way in offering pre-need products. Pre-need plans are being aggressively sold in the consumer's home, by phone and through the mail.
Recordings	A growing trend among funeral directors is to offer a video or audio tape of the service. The premise behind this new marketing twist is to be able to share the event with family members unable to attend the service. If this appeals to you, there may be a good friend of the family that would do it for you at no cost.
Refrigeration	A means of maintaining a deceased body until a decision has been made as to the type of disposition of the body. The charges for this service are usually on a per-day basis. Refrigeration is

sometimes used in lieu of embalming in order to comply with state laws.

Regulations

It is illegal to tell consumers that federal, state or local laws require them to purchase any specific goods or services when that is not the case. If, however, there is such a law or requirement, it is the responsibility of the funeral director to identify and describe the law or requirement and furnish a copy of the same to the consumer.

Receiving Remains from Another Funeral Home

This is a service that the funeral home would charge to receive the body from out of state. These charges should be clearly stated on the funeral home's General Price List.

Restoration

There is usually an extra charge by funeral homes when an autopsy has been performed on the body. In the case of accidents when viewing is requested as part of the funeral service, the funeral director will perform restorative artistry to rebuild a facial injury or any part of the body that will be visible.

Rental Casket

Used for funeral services followed by a cremation. Usually a hardwood casket with the bottom out that slips over a plastic liner or cardboard insert that holds the deceased. The deceased is then transported to the crematory in the plastic liner or insert following the funeral service.

Revocable Trust

Set up so that the money **CAN BE** removed from the trust at any time.

Rigor Mortis

The body becomes stiff, when the lungs stop functioning, the cells of the muscles can only operate anaerobically and the lactic acid builds up. Over a short period of time, this lactic acid buildup turns to a gelatinous consistency that results in stiffening of the body.

Scatter Cremains

Could be by airplane, ship or rose garden in the cemetery and in some states on the mountaintop.

SCI

Service Corporation International. The largest of all funeral home and cemetery conglomerates, based out of Houston, Texas. In 1997 SCI owned 3,012 funeral homes, 365 cemeteries and 156 crematoriums in the United States, Canada, England, France and other countries. *December, 1997, Mortuary Management Magazine.*

Statement of Funeral Goods Selected	This is an itemized list of all goods and services and their prices that the consumer has selected. It is illegal for the funeral director or aggregate to combine costs on the **Statement** that are listed separately on the General Price List. It also provides the consumer with detailed information on any cemetery or crematory requirements that require the purchase of any specific funeral goods or services and to review the decisions made and their corresponding costs.

The Funeral Rule further requires the funeral director to give consumers the **Statement** at the end of the arrangement meeting, and is a violation of the Rule to give the **Statement** to the consumer at the funeral or at a later date. If the arrangements were made over the telephone, it is incumbent upon the funeral director to get a copy of the **Statement** to the consumer at the earliest possible moment. |
Use of Facilities and Staff for Funeral or Memorial Services	There should be only one charge for facilities and staff when a funeral service or memorial service is held at the funeral home. There should only be a charge for staff for funerals held at another location; i.e., church, synagogue, clubhouse. etc.
Somatic Death	The point when a person ceases to breathe and the heart no longer beats.
Stationery	Guest registers, announcement cards, prayer cards, thank you cards, a memorial register book and acknowledgement notes all provided by the funeral director or purchased for less by yourself elsewhere.
Stewart Enterprises	One of the big three funeral conglomerates headquartered in Metairie, Louisiana. In 1997 Stewart owned 378 funeral homes, 127 cemeteries in twenty-three states, Puerto Rico, Mexico, Australia, New Zealand, Canada, Spain and Portugal. **November, 1997, Mortuary Management Magazine**
Thanatologists	Experts on death.
Totten Trust	It is a savings plan that is controlled by the consumer. Available in every state. If you elect to cancel the trust, all principle and interest is returned.

Trust Funds	A pre-funded trust account that can be used to cover funeral goods and services for a future date. In most cases these plans do not guarantee the consumer that the funds invested will actually cover the cost of the funeral.
Utility Car	A service or utility vehicle used for many different services by the funeral home. These vehicles are used in making removals of the deceased from the place of death, as a flower car, as a car to transport the minister or priest to the cemetery. You will normally pay extra for this vehicle as well as the hearse or limousine.
Vault	A completely enclosed box usually made of reinforced concrete and sometimes coated with asphalt mix and more recently plastic (polypropylene) and fiberglass vaults. Vaults can also be made of steel, either galvanized or non-galvanized, from 10 to 12 gauge in thickness. Vaults are lined with metal, fiberglass or plastic.
Viewing Charges	Either a flat fee or an hourly rate may be charged for this item. The cost of facilities and staff should be included in one charge unless the viewing is held away from the funeral home, in which case there should be no charge for facilities.
Visitation	Usually a time set aside for viewing the deceased prior to the funeral service. It can be private, for the family only, open or closed casket. Flowers can be sent and family and friends can sign a memorial register book. The funeral home will charge for each day of visitation.
Wake	An annual English parish festival formerly held in commemoration of the church's patron saint. A watch held over the body of a dead person prior to burial and sometimes accompanied by festivity.
Urn	Containers for the cremated remains, (ashes). They come in many different sizes and shapes, and they are made from glass, ceramic, bronze and other materials.

Other Resources

"The American Way of Death," Jessica Mitford, 1963,333 pages (famous expose book about the funeral industry.)

"The High Cost of Death," Ruth Harmer, 1963 256 pages (another famous expose book about the funeral industry.)

"The Cost of Dying and What You Can Do about It," Raymond Arvio, 1974 (Starting co-op mortuaries.)

"Funerals: Consumers' Last Rights," Consumers Union, 1977,334 pages

"Caring for Your Own Dead, a Final Act of Love," Lisa Carlson, 1987, 343 pages

"Funeral Industry Practices—Final Staff Report, Proposed Amended Trade Regulation Rule," Federal Trade Commission, Washington, DC June 1990 (report on the 1988-89 FTC hearings on the effect of the 1984 Funeral Rule regulation.)

"Products Reports"
    "Funeral Goods and Services"
    "Pre-Paying Your Funeral"
    "Cemetery Goods and Services"
    Prepaying your Funeral: Some Questions to Ask"
Free from: American Association of Retired Persons (AARP), Washington, DC, 1992.

"Dealing Creatively With Death: A Manual of Death Education," Ernest Morgan, 13 edition, 1994.

"Understanding the Tricks of the Funeral Trade: Self Defense for Consumers," Lisa Carlson, 1995, Funeral and Memorial Societies of America (FAMSA)